WOODSTOCK
CRAFTSMAN'S
MANUAL

Books Provoked by Jean Young
    Woodstock Craftsman's Manual

Books by Jean Young and Jim Young
    The Garage Sale Manual
    People's Guide to Country Real Estate (forthcoming)

WOODSTOCK CRAFTSMAN'S MANUAL 2

provoked by Jean Young

PRAEGER PUBLISHERS

New York • Washington

The quotation on page 133 is taken from <u>Black Elk Speaks</u> by John G. Neilhardt. Permission by courtesy of the author and Simon & Schuster Publishing Company.

BOOKS THAT MATTER

Published in the United States of America in 1973
by Praeger Publishers, Inc.
111 Fourth Avenue, New York, N.Y. 10003·

<u>Second printing, 1973</u>

Library of Congress Catalog Card Number: 72-92472

Cover and book design by Jean Young
Photographs, except when otherwise acknowledged, by Jean Young

Printed in the United States of America

Woodstock Roots 2

Here is an extension of the first Manual, written by craftspeople who live in Woodstock, New York. Their voices are fresh with the spirit of a new age in crafts. For them there are no academies, no sexist <u>his</u> and <u>her</u> crafts, no trite projects. They have done much to eliminate the psychological block of thinking in terms of beginning, intermediate, and advanced.

The freedom is here, I think, to allow you to get together with the people and close to their crafts. They don't harness you with designs to copy; they encourage you to find your own feelings so you have the concentrated satisfaction of making something real. All you need is the ability to read to get on with these authors.

My reason for putting together these books with more crafts is that today our vitality demands more than an unquestioned allegiance to a single pursuit. It used to be that a weaver was a weaver was a weaver, but today a weaver is a songwriter, is a silversmith, is a tipi-maker, is a media freak. The whole earth is a whole life of multi-experiences.

Thanks to True Light Beaver/Alan Carey for the photographs in <u>Making Media</u> and the photograph of Sandee Shaw in <u>Bronzeworking</u>; to <u>Arnie Abrams</u> for the <u>Needlepoint</u> photographs; to Woody Woodriff, who is shown making sandals in the <u>Sandalmaking</u> chapter; to Rick Brightfield for the borders in <u>Songwriting</u> and <u>How to Write a Song</u>; to Glory Brightfield for borders in <u>Tipi-Making</u>; to Shelagh Young for illustrating <u>Tipi-Making</u> and <u>Sandalmaking</u>; to Terry Fowler for typing; to Bill Reed for his nine-to-five; to Michael Green, whose cover for the first book inspired the second cover design; to Peter Grant for his help with <u>Stained Glass</u>; and to Ellyn Childs, Ferol Sibley Warthen, Kyle King, Yvonne Outen, Jim Young, and all the authors who did their own illustrations.

Jean Young

Crafts

People

WOODSTOCK CRAFTSMAN'S MANUAL

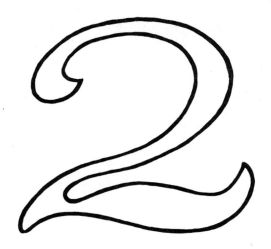

Patchwork
Appliqué
Quilting

Carol W. Abrams

Grandmother's quilt was a cave, warm and silent, hiding me from a fluorescent, clattering world where pimples, thick glasses, and big feet were unacceptable. There I would snuggle, flashlight and book in hand, succeeding often in extending the bedtime hour, invisible save for the massive lump in the center of the bed. Time never existed as I lay dreaming and toasting in the stuffy warmth of the old cover, the world outside a memory. Ah, that quilt—it wasn't a fancy patchwork delicacy, nor was it a marvel of appliqué and sewing wizardry. It was a solid, useful, heavy quilt, copper-colored on one side, functional brown on the other, six inches thick and very big.

Since then I have barely grown accustomed to the fluorescence, the noise, the masses of people. Like many poorly adjusted urbanites, I seek security in the past. Quilting has become a symbol of that past, that security. A quilt fosters a feeling of calm connectedness with people who had time to touch personally all that surrounded them. It is to these craftswomen I give my deepest thanks for giving me and others a chance to enjoy their labors.

There are many kinds of quilts and quilting techniques. The term "quilting" is misleading. It is a catchall word for appliqué and patchwork and is used in conjunction with these as well as on its own. Quilting is the final process of finishing a patchwork or appliquéd top and turning these humble pieces of cloth into plush, warm, rich blankets, feasts for the eyes and body. The simple sewing of a back, some stuffing, and a patterned top of scraps and pieces became a glorious and involving craft ... no, an art. Yes, art rivaling bas-relief. Patterns, scrolls, feathers, flowers, birds, geometrics, ropes, symbols, and signs have all been the subjects of the quilter's needles. The cold-fingered colonial and pioneer women, gathered in their fire rooms, gossiping and passing news, turned the dreary, necessary task of making bed clothing into an expression of beauty as well as welcome warmth on those bitter winter nights.

Piecework quilts, made of snips and chunks of discarded clothing and scraps remaining from sewing projects, were frugally cut and fitted into ingenious patterns with never a precious piece wasted. Some old patterns have pieces so small that many now would think it foolish to worry about such bits. In this age of inflation, we could learn much from those thrifty craftspeople: the idea of recycling material is far from a new one.

Patchwork, the technique most people think of in connection with quilting, is the same as piecework, except that instead of snips and scraps you use fabric specifically set aside for the purpose. Piecework and patchwork are actually so indistinguishable on any other level that it isn't worth the time quibbling—I will refer to both here as patchwork (you must admit it's easier than "patchwork or piecework"). Use both methods when you get involved—combine scraps you have around (finally you'll have a way to use that size-38, man-tailored shirt Cousin Isadora sent you for your nineteenth birthday) and fill out the collection with purchased stuff. Don't stand on ceremony, piece your patchwork or patch your piecework.

Appliqué is the ultimate in extravagance in quilting by comparison with patchwork. This technique is widely used by the Pennsylvania Dutch, who have perfected the art of quilting (though it's by no means the only technique they use). Sewing one piece of fabric onto another larger piece in a pattern is appliqué. Odds and ends from other sewing projects, or unworn pieces of old clothes, can be used as successfully here as with patchwork. Delicate scrolls and arches, circles and gentle curves, leaves, flowers, imaginative medallions, and other forms are all possible with appliqué, unlike patchwork, which is for practical purposes limited to straight seams. Though skilled patchworkers are able to handle very gradual curves, appliqué affords greater flexibility in design.

Both of these methods are exciting and offer possibilities that can harness the creative energies of even the most stubborn pragmatist. Imagine producing an object, useful and welcome, a grand addition to any lifestyle, adding warmth to rented flats far from home or adding that "personal" touch to professionally decorated places. Beauty and utility are interchangeable and indistinguishable when you surround yourself with a quilt of your own handicraft.

PATCHWORK

PATTERNS:

Forward, I say, and on to the nitty-gritty. Like everything else, if you haven't any experience but want to try, <u>start small</u>—a patch, a purse, a pocket—wherever your head takes you. Just whittle the following directions down to size. What shall I use as a pattern, you ask. Well, says I, anything as long as it fits into a square. There are many sources for patterns; dig out of those dusty library archives some Italian Gothic ornaments, Mohammedan designs, Byzantine folk-art patterns, Arabian floor and textile patterns. Go to your nearest toy box and take out the wooden blocks and play around with them—as tempting as it may be to build towers and go boom, try to use them as pattern builders for patches. There are many old books around of classic American patterns specifically for quilts. Maybe your grandmother has a few. You will soon want to design your own. If you're new at quilting, pick an easy pattern.

Random or Crazy Quilt patterns use schnitzels of fabric, all and any shape and size, sewn together to fit into squares. These may have been the first attempt by a needleworker to make a larger cloth from a smaller cloth. Maybe a blanket was so old and so patched that it inspired the "crazy" pattern.

By far the easiest patchwork is simply sewing squares of cloth in rows or brick-fashion. This is a very old "one-patch" pattern. Thin strips of cloth sewn into ribbons and laid in alternating light and dark stripes is an old pattern called Roman Stripes. Hexagons, rectangles, triangles have all been used for one-patch patterns. These one-patches produce soothing all-over textured patterns that were obviously the grandmothers of all the patterns in America. Great things can be done with color and fabric combinations here.

   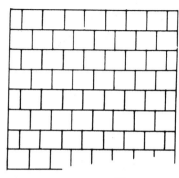

Rows   Bricks

Three-patch patterns are also simple, and the next step from one-patch. The striking (yuk, yuk) Streak o' Lightning, in which light and dark triangles are set together, is a form of this primitive pattern.

I Square of cloth folded on line in direction of arrows

II Cut along dotted line from opposite corners

III Unfold and put aside corner pieces for future use

IV Stitch two equilateral triangles together

V Completed quilt top

"Streak O' Lightning"

The most familiar and varied patterns for patchwork are the numerous four- and nine-patch patterns, all based on the folding and cutting of a square into three or four parts.

Diamond patterns can open up many more possibilities for effective and beautiful patches, though they are more time-consuming to make than plain squares. Middle-Eastern, Moorish, and Oriental geometrical designs have a very fine comrade in American diamond-patch patterns.

As kids we would cut from colored paper six- and eight-pointed stars, snowflakes, and lacy geometrics on dreary afternoons. We could create a snowstorm in July or a starry summer night on a drizzly November day. Little did I know these patterns, so easy and beautiful, were the basis for many, many impressive patches: Lemon Star, Carpenter's Wheel, Sunburst, etc. Here's a chance to mess around as if you were eight again, and have a productive time of it. Newspaper, construction paper, brown paper—whatever you have on hand—and a pair of long-bladed scissors are all you need. Using colored construction or two different kinds of plain paper gives you a chance to visualize colors in a completed pattern or relationship of light and dark. In the old days quilts made for the spring and fall had lightweight filling and a color scheme of spring white and fall colors. They have a nice dark-and-light effect.

The paper should be 14 to 18 inches square. A big square is more fun than a little square. The square you choose will be the size of one cloth patch when finished. Fold the square into three or four parts. Make straight cuts through all the layers of paper and see what you come up with.

Folds

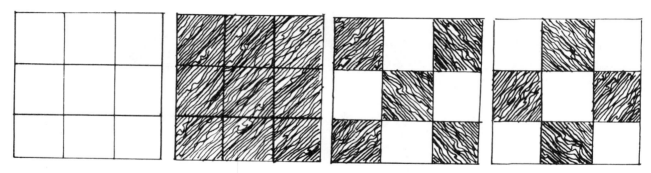

Interchanging pieces

Cut two or three of the same shape from different papers and interchange the pieces with one another. This is the basis of all patchwork. If you don't like what you've come up with, try again until you do. Keep in mind that all the seams (cuts) should be straight, for ease in sewing, especially if you are a novice. Concave and convex forms are tough to fit to make the patch come out perfectly square later. Save the fancy curves for appliqué. There are many classic patterns relying on curves—Orange Peel, Drunkard's Path, Dresden Plate, Rob-Peter-to-Pay-Paul—so don't put them out of your mind completely. I am just advising discretion.

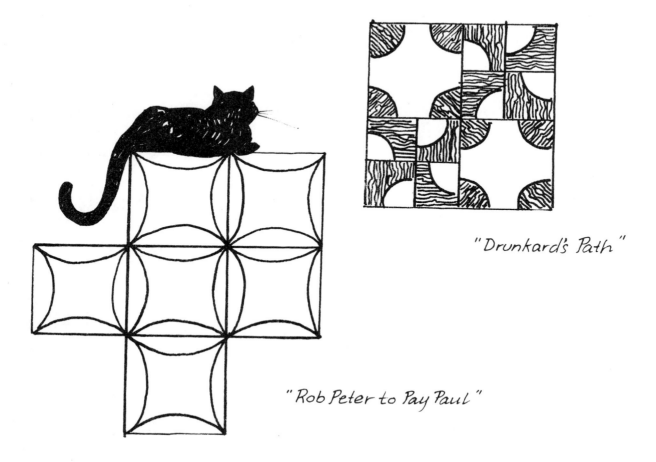

"Drunkard's Path"

"Rob Peter to Pay Paul"

Fold in direction of arrows along dotted line

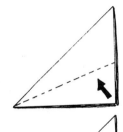

Right angles, squares, isosceles triangles, equilateral- and right-triangle rectangles, and parallelograms are all pure forms, and any number of unique patterns can be worked up by using them in conjunction with one another. It's one great and fascinating puzzle.

Folding a square to make a six-pointed or eight-pointed star is easy. The eight-pointed star is a real gas to play with; as the angles between the points form a right angle they can be used easily with squares and right triangles.

Cut along "A-B" through all layers

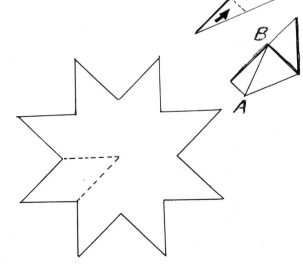

Once you find the forms you like, make pattern "templates" of them out of flexible bristol board, cutting them with precision. Record your patterns full size in a notebook or drawing pad as reference for future quilts and as an insurance against the loss of your templates. Write on each template the number of times you'll need to cut that shape out of cloth to complete each kind of patch you are planning to use. All the pieces must fit precisely together "as accurately as a baby's puzzle," one of my teachers has said. This is the time to assure yourself of that accuracy. You can build quite a collection of templates to use over and over again. Our grandmothers and great-grandmothers would exchange their patterns, each user adding her own touch. Histories can be written tracing familiar old European patterns as they moved through colonial, pioneer, Victorian, and turn-of-the-century changes, and there is always room for more; an original pattern is prized above all else. In this day of extended leisure time, and with the need to touch once again all that surrounds us, patchwork and all forms of handwork are welcome.

FABRICS:

Broadcloth, men's shirt fabrics (especially the new bright prints), muslin, fine linen, percale, cambric, polished cotton, good old gingham, and, of course, calico and chintz are fine for a washable, usable product, whether it be for appliqué or patchwork. Old sheets with bright patterns and colors are perfect. Baby clothes and old shirts and dresses are good for patches. Wools, silks, velours, velvets, and satins are excellent, and very plush for patchwork. These require some experience to handle and should be steered clear of by the novice. This age of permanent press can be a boon to the quilter, though many prefer to stick to the original natural cottons and linens and wools used by the early quilters. The rougher, wrinkly surface of these fabrics lend a certain charm that the synthetics can't offer. You must go where your head takes you. I use anything I can get my hands on that will work well with my patterns, as long as the fabrics are of comparable weight and composition.

If you are hard up for scraps, hunt through the closets and boxes

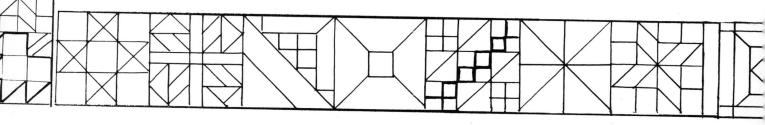

around the place. This is a good excuse for cleaning out the attic. One veteran quilter I know goes to the Salvation Army or similar outlets and buys old clothes to cut up for patches. Neighbors, friends, and relatives are also good sources. This was the way scraps were latched on to by the early quilters. It must have been fascinating to go over the patches: "This is granny's wedding dress, sister's christening robe, great-grandfather's best Sunday suit..." Imagine the future: "This is grandma's jeans she wore at her lib meetings, sister's workshirt she wore in the Chicago riots, great-grandfather's best meditation toga..."

If you are buying material for your quilt, measure the surface you anticipate covering (i.e., bed, pillow). Add a few inches for seams and translate into yardage. This will cover your backing. With full-size paper patterns of your basic patch blocks determine how many patches you will be using to cover the surface of your quilt; in order to complete the design, some blocks must be sewn side by side; others can be framed with strips of fabric or interspersed checkerboard fashion with plain fabric blocks (squares). Account for a border also if you want one. You should have an idea now of how much basic fabric you'll be needing to cover the back, and the borders and blank blocks if you are using any. Once these decisions are made you'll know the number of patch blocks. You have already marked each template with the number of times it will have to be used to complete each basic patch block. Trace the template that many times on a large sheet of paper, placing each tracing at right angles to the paper's edge as you would on fabric. Group those to be cut from the same fabric together. Leave at least 1/2-inch on all sides of each tracing. Repeat this process for all the templates to be used to complete the block. With a straight-edged ruler, measure the areas each set of templates occupies on the paper. Treat the templates of the same type that will be cut from the same fabric as one set. Multiply these sets by the number of patches required to complete the quilt. Convert the number you get into yardage. You will have the amount of fabric needed for each fabric used in all the patches. Be generous—better too much stuff than too little. This process may sound a little like the "house that Jack built." Take it slow and it will work every time.

As an example, let's choose this block for the top of the quilt. We will use it six times to complete the design (this is an arbitrary number, the number of times you will use a block is up to you.)

It takes three templates to make up the block chosen. I have shown the templates cut out of cardboard and marked on them the number of times each will be used to complete one block.

On a large sheet of paper trace one of the templates the number of times it will be used from one type of fabric (lay the templates, as you would on the fabric, at right angles to the sides, leaving a generous 1/2-inch between each tracing for the seam allowances).

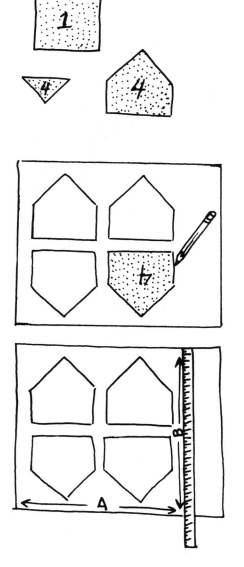

With a ruler or tapemeasure measure the width and length of the area occuped by the template tracings. Multiply side A by side B and you will have the number of square inches of fabric one set of pieces from one template will require. Then multiply that number by the number of times you will be using the complete block on the surface of your quilt (in this case we decided to use this block six times, so multiply by six). From this you will derive the number of square inches of fabric you will need all together for all the pieces cut from the same fabric from one template.

Repeat this whole process for each template.

Convert the total number of square inches into yards of fabric you will need (see chart). I usually add a safety margin of at least 1/2-yard to give me room to manipulate the pieces and allow for errors.

There are:
1296 square inches per yard of 36=inch-wide fabric

1620 square inches per yard of 45=inch-wide fabric

1872 square inches per yard of 52=inch-wide fabric

If you are using scraps, there's no way to tell you how much of what cloth you'll be needing, obviously. But that's the fun of it. You'll still have to figure out your backings, borders, and empty blocks as before, though. Unless you are lucky and have enough stuff around, you'll have to purchase that much fabric at least. Group your scraps together by color instead of by pattern, as it is most likely you will have more scraps similar in color than in pattern. That way you will know what colors you have most of and which one will dominate. There are no set formulas for any of this, it all depends upon what you have available to you at the time. You can make each patch complete in its own color scheme, with the pattern determining how they will be coordinated; or you can disperse your colors evenly through-out the quilt. A quilt whose pattern is made of scraps is a lot like people; the pattern is the same but the fabric each individual patch is made from determines its character. Within one quilt each patch could be different— bold and bright, soft and quiet, crazily mixed up, darkly somber, subtly textured, or sunny and light.

CUTTING AND MAKING PATCHES:

Your templates are made, your fabric is together, and you are ready to begin. With these, a pencil, iron and ironing board, <u>sharp</u> scissors with long blades (notice the emphasis on sharp), and a lap-size board or table, with a good light, you are ready to cut your pieces. Whether you are making a bed-size quilt or a single patch you must organize yourself. Even though you are not instrument-flying, try and repeat to yourself "precision and accuracy," "precision and accuracy," "precision and accuracy," throughout this whole trip. This is where it counts. All pieces must be cut accurately so they fit precisely together to avoid unnecessary pulling and puckering later.

Wash all new fabric before you begin. It removes stiff sizing and shrinks it now—not later, after the quilt is completed. Check also to see if the fabric's color runs. Wow, could that be messy!

You had better have a reasonable relationship with your iron, as you'll be seeing a lot of it from now on. Press all fabric smooth. Spread the fabric, <u>front side down</u>, on the lap-board or table. With the longest part of the template running along the length of the fabric parallel to the selvages (the warp, or bound sides), trace the template as you did on paper once before. Use a sharp pencil, sharpening it as you go if necessary. A two-degree variation in some patterns can distort the entire quilt's surface. Repeat "precision and accuracy," as you carefully trace all the pieces you'll need. Leave 1/2-inch between each tracing—a generous 1/2-inch at that—as this is your seam allowance. If you are using a patterned cloth, make sure your template tracings are all running in the same direction to assure evenness and symmetry in all the patches. Repeat "precision and accuracy." Now, relax, go for a walk, flip on the FM, or just have a leisurely cup of tea before moving on to the next step. Have a friend over so you can brag about how well you are doing.

Cutting pieces for a patch block

BACK of FABRIC

CUTTING LINE

PENCIL

TEMPLATE

1/4"

TRIM CORNERS

Carefully cut around the pencil lines, leaving 1/4-inch excess as a seam allowance. The pencil line becomes your seam line. White blackboard chalk or French tailor's chalk can be used on dark fabrics if pencil won't show. The chalk should make a thin, fine line for reasons already stated. Use sandpaper or emery board to keep the chalk sharp. Pencil is better if you can possibly manage it. Remember "precision and accuracy."

Cut all the pieces for all the patches now so that, should you be short on fabric, you will have a better chance of matching it. Use a lap-size board while sitting in a comfortable chair. This makes cutting very pleasant, especially if the chair is on the front porch of an old farm-type house. Breathe in the good air (pretend, can't you?) and really experience this homely task. Consider the past, look to the future. Become one with yourself and the world. The board gives you a place to spread the fabric with its tracings out in front of you. Sort the pieces, either by color and shape or by complete patch. If you are using scraps but have definite ideas about what you want in color and pattern put the pieces for a whole patch together. Otherwise sorting by shape is convenient, so that you can grab a piece when you need it. Safety-pin them together whichever way you sort them. Just don't lose any. Man, that would be disastrous if you had no more fabric — just think.

After traveling along this long arduous road, you are now prepared to stitch the pieces together. You'll need your iron again, a short, sharp needle, and white (it's stronger) mercerized cotton. A good light, a comfortable chair, a crackling fire or your favorite "soap," or some good conversation with a good friend provides a really fine atmosphere in which to complete each patch. Remove two pieces that are placed next to one another in your pattern from their pins and press them if they are wrinkled. Put them face to face with the sides that correspond together. The pencil lines

Stitching the pieces

27

are the lines that you will be stitching on, using small, neat running stitches. Knot your thread to start and, at the end of each seam, backstitch once or twice to finish. Make sure your needle is piercing the pencil lines on both pieces of fabric so that they will fit perfectly together. Repeat "precision and accuracy."

Running stitch   Arrow represents needle → thread
Use this stitch — longer — for basting "B-E": knotting off at completion

Press these pieces lightly, flattening the seam to one side. Repeat the stitching process with the next adjoining piece. Finish seaming various sections of the pattern first, then join them together, overcasting the corners where they join. Try to be accurate. "Precision and accuracy" is truer here than anywhere else. In no time your patch should be complete. Iron it lightly from the back, pressing all the seams over to one side.

Press seams to one side

Overcasting Corners

BLOCKING:

Blocking means simply pressing the patchwork block so that it will lie square. You'll need, once more, your ironing board, or, better still, a table, or board larger than your block, with a couple of layers of towels and a sheet or pillowcase thrown over it. Pin down the patchwork block with the corners square. Use a right angle of some sort—a protractor or carpenter's angle; don't eyeball it, that's too inaccurate. Stretch and pin the piece securely and lay a damp cloth over it. Press smooth, starting from the edges and working to the middle. That way you don't stretch and distort the edges. Ironing the block dry is a no-no. Steaming is the key, and a steam iron is even better. You are only trying to set the block straight, not dry the living daylights out of it. Let the block cool off a minute before removing it from the board so it won't stretch while it is still damp and hot. Blocking will be the test for your "precision and accuracy" sessions. If you have laid and cut your pieces accurately, sewn precisely on the pencil lines, pressed the pieces all along—then there will be no problems. If not, then your difficulties will show. Doom and gloom—puckered seams (too tight stitching), pulling corners (inaccurate cutting, tsk, tsk), separating seams (too loose stitching or seams that weren't flattened to one side), lopsided fittings—doom and gloom. You've learned though, and should try again. Most likely none of these things will have happened at all (if you were thinking about what you were doing).

SETTING AND SEAMING:

Now the blocks are prepared to be "set" together. This is a quaint term meaning fitting and sewing together the blocks and any strips or blank blocks that are used to connect your patchwork blocks. When all your blocks of patchwork are complete, lay them out and admire them. Arrange them in the order that you want. Check out the total measurements again and adjust the borders and connecting bands, if you'll have any. If you had decided to lay out a checkerboard-type quilt with every other block blank, check to see if the blank blocks correspond in size to your patched blocks. Adjust the seam allowances now. Pat yourself on the back. Brag a little. You've come this far and the rest is a downhill trip, coasting all the way.

A few variations on quilt sets

I like to do all my seams by hand. I enjoy it. Seam the blocks together using neat running stitches, overcasting corners as before. If you've decided to use a sewing machine, adjust the stitch length to a bit longer than the one ordinarily used for the type of fabric you're using. The seams won't be so pinched after quilting. For a quilt with borders around each block, add the shorter borders, on the top and bottom first. For the long vertical borders connecting these strips of blocks and borders, basting first is recommended, even if you are using a machine. Stitch as before. Repeat until the top is done. Press the whole surface from the back checking that all the seams are secure and flat to one side.

HALLELUIAH! It's time to quilt.

But first a word about appliqué.

APPLIQUÉ

Lush primordial ferns, rich lazy feathers, weird birds, and all sorts of exotic flora and fauna have been spread over quilt tops in appliqué for centuries. Fantastic wreaths of roses, strawberries on vines of laurel leaves, eagles, farmhouses, grapes—almost anything the mind could conjure was used. Appliqué gives the needleworker a chance to experience long continuous curves, jagged shapes, tiny circles, and complicated forms. Things that patchwork couldn't offer.

The appliquéd top is usually worked in blocks, much the same as patchwork. But instead of building a block of fabric from smaller pieces, you sew fabric pieces cut in shapes onto a solid fabric block. Pattern inspirations are all around us—hands, kaleidoscopes, Busby Berkeley movies, your mother's old crystal, food, circuses, gardens, traffic signs—

anything can be converted into a pattern appliqué. If you've patched a pair of jeans you've appliquéd.

The principles, procedures, and measurements are almost the same as for patchwork—the pattern worked up, templates cut, fabric needs determined. The only real difference is that the templates do not have to fit precisely together, as you are not fitting a block from the pieces. One appliqué extra you may want to put on your shopping list is bias tape. More about this later.

Cut-paper patterns are fun, and those used for patchwork can easily be adapted to appliqué. Cut curves, holes, petal forms, snowflakes, old-fashioned hearts, Art Nouveau forms—see what you get. If you want geometrics or patterns that are symmetrical, fold paper and cut much as before. Don't get too terribly involved (especially at first) with intricacies, doodads, and tiny little shapes, as tempting as that may be (they are difficult to sew down, anyway). Bold simple shapes are easier to handle. Canadian multimedia artist Joyce Wieland designed a huge, wall-hanging quilt using the cool, sensual lines of Canadian landscapes, each block containing a different pattern and each block a different size. There are things that surround us that can be beautifully worked up into intriguing patterns. Look around, become aware, the world is beautiful.

When you have found something you like, trace it out on large sheets of paper. Paint or color it with crayons or cut it from colored paper and see what relationships develop (remembering, of course, that your fabric colors will only approximate the pattern's painted ones).

Cut your cardboard templates.

A review of what was covered in the previous section: First, measure the amount of backing material you will need, allowing for seams around the edges. Then, measure the amount of base fabric you'll need to cover the top. You can do this by simply doubling the amount you need for the backing, if you choose to leave it whole and appliqué over the entire top. This is especially effective for large bold central designs. On the other hand, you can cut the top up into blocks; if you plan to do this, remember to add extra for the seams you'll need to join them together. Blocks are easier than trying to manipulate yards of fabric all at once. I can't sit with an 8- or 10-foot-wide piece of cloth and try to stitch a 3-inch by 4-inch shape to it without a little frustration. Many needleworkers carry it off beautifully and with little trouble, so obviously it isn't impossible. Now, measure the amount of fabric you'll need for your appliqué pattern by again tracing all your templates and measuring the tracing areas for each fabric you'll be using. Record your templates in a notebook, as suggested for patchwork. I encourage this because more than once my cats have taken great delight in chewing up my templates and leaving their sodden punctured remains all over my work place. So rather than eliminate the cats, or lock my templates up, I simply retrace them from my notebook. (Cats, as I'm sure you realize, aren't the only threat to templates.)

So, you've designed a pattern, cut your templates, figured the fabric yardage you need for the back, top, and the borders and the pattern (avoiding stretchy or sleazy fabrics), and have your trusty iron, sharp scissors, table or cutting board, and sharp pencils on hand. You are now ready to begin. Make sure you are working in a comfortable well-lit environment. Baroque recorder music might be a soothing accompaniment.

Carefully trace the templates on the back of the fabric, leaving a generous 1/2-inch between each tracing. Cut and sort the pieces as described for patchwork. Mistakes made cost time and material. Once again, each piece should be ironed and this time the edges should be turned under 1/4-inch. If you find that you are singeing your fingers in the process then crease the edge under as you would fold paper, between your fingers. Most fabrics will cooperate, at least until you can press the edges down with the iron. Use the pencil line as the fold line so the pieces conform to the templates. On deep curves, convex or concave, clip the seam allowance to ease the strain. Don't cut through the penciled seam line or it will show on the piece's surface as a slash and will ravel and fray. Ugly, ugly. You might even run a basting stitch or a very long machine stitch right on the pencil line before folding the seam allowance under. This seems to ease folding. Baste the folded edge down with a contrasting colored thread and long running stitches. Keep your knots on top so you can just clip them off and pull out the thread when the appliqué is complete. Sort the pieces and pin them together with long safety pins, and move on.

TEMPLATE

BACK of FABRIC

Find the center of your block by folding it into equal quarters. This helps lay out the pattern evenly, especially if it is symmetrical. Lay your pattern pieces out on the base block in the order you wish to complete the pattern. You may even wish to transfer an outline of the whole pattern onto the base block with transfer pencil, dressmaker's carbon, or chalk. Then all you have to do is stick the right pieces onto the right shape, sort of like the "cut and paste" stickers that Uncle Dan gave you for Christmas (even though you were almost eighteen). Baste the pieces down to the block in contrasting thread, overlapping sections appropriately (stems behind flowers, etc.). Then sew the pattern down with super-neat appliqué stitches, keeping the pieces and base block as smooth and flat as possible. Use white thread or a color to coordinate with the pieces. Most appliquéers sew the pieces down by hand with the base blocks in their laps or on a table. I like to use a 10-inch standing embroidery hoop or the larger standing quilting hoop, depending upon the size of the base block. You might want to try it. It gives a nice smooth finish and frees both hands for stitching. Mount your base block in the hoop so the surface is smooth. Don't over-stretch it by making the fabric too tight or you'll have just what you didn't want—puckering. Neatly appliqué the pieces to the surface and, if you didn't stretch the base too tight, you'll have a very professional-looking product. As you can see, I discourage very stretchy fabrics (though every fabric will stretch some), because there is less control of surface tension with them.

Basting

Appliqué stitch should be very tiny -- almost invisible.

If you have a pattern with pieces less than 1 inch wide, then bias tape can be used very comfortably, giving you the chance to avoid having to cut such thin schnitzels of cloth. You can purchase this ready-made in any well-stocked notions department, or you can make it out of the fabric used for the rest of your pieces. I like making it. It's therapeutic. This way you wind up with a perfectly coordinated appliqué at less expense. Bias strips can also be used for binding the completed quilt's edges. You must account for these things when you purchase the fabric for your project. Gad, it is frustrating to have bias stripping that goes all around the quilt ... almost. To make bias strips, pull a thread running from one selvage to the other on each cut edge of a piece of the fabric. (This ensures that the warp and weft of the fabric are at right angles to each other.) Fold the fabric so that the selvage of one side runs along the pulled thread line of the adjacent perpendicular side. With a long straight-edge (a metal-edged ruler is perfect) laid diagonally on the fold as in the illustration, draw parallel lines about 1 inch or 1-1/2 inch wide with a pencil. With sharp scissors cut the lines. Press under the edges of each strip to make the right width.

To use bias stripping or commercial bias tape on straight lines is easy; just baste down and appliqué. To use it on curved lines, baste the <u>inside</u> of the curve first, then appliqué, baste, and stitch the outside of the curve last. This way, the tape has a chance to stretch into place without the interior curves puckering. Believe me, it really works.

Making bias strips

When the pattern is complete on a base block, you should block it by pinning it to the ironing board and pressing it with a damp cloth in the same manner described for patchwork. Work gently—avoid stretching. Press from the center out to the sides, unlike the sides-to-the-center method for patchwork. Appliqué presses much smoother this way. When all the blocks are completed and ready to be set together, lay them out and make all the necessary adjustments and considerations now. They will be breathtakingly gorgeous, right? Set and seam the completed blocks together, checkerboard, strips and borders, angles... whatever you feel suits your pattern best.

One more time: HALLELUIAH! It is time to quilt.

...almost.

If you have chosen an elaborate patchwork pattern with very little negative (empty or blank) space in it you'll not have to fuss too much with quilting patterns (the linear patterns the quilting stitching makes), as the patchwork becomes the major part of your quilting pattern. If you have chosen to make a top with alternate blocks of pattern and space (checkerboard), quilting patterns must be considered and chosen. Most appliqué tops have quite a bit of negative space. There again patterns must be selected. It is here your imagination can run wild. Quilting patterns are much like a pebble thrown in water. The many concentric rings form the pattern. Quilting patterns are just a stone thrown in water that refused to throw up concentric rings—instead there are concentric forms of all sorts, ropes, waves, feather forms, geometric forms, and so many more.

Quilting is simply the sewing together of a top, some stuffing, and a back or bottom. Sounds simple, right? Wrong. Sure, you can just stitch the three layers together so they don't slip, but if you are going to invest

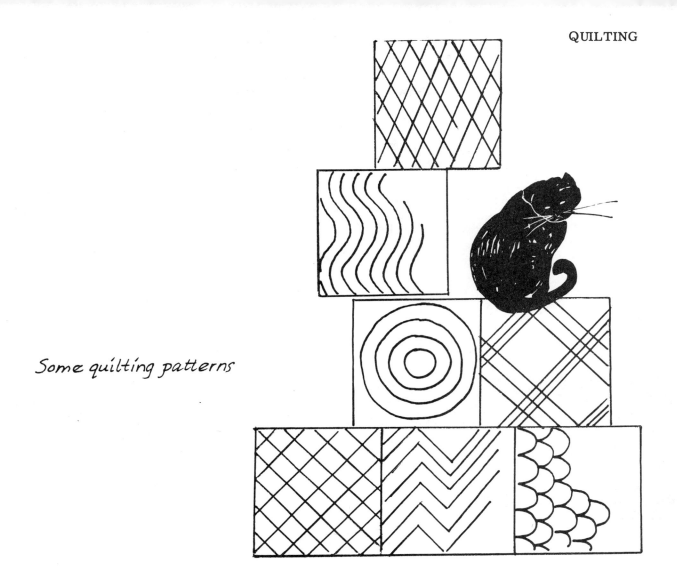

Some quilting patterns

all that time in just stitching them together, why not make it an exciting creative experience? So far, patchwork or appliqué has been more than creating big things from little things or sticking one piece of cloth onto another. Quilting the top to its stuffing and backing can also become more than just stitching together. Some of the more expressive antique patterns for quilting were ferns, wreaths, feathers, feathers, feathers, plant forms, fan forms, geometric forms, and pineapples (yeah, pineapples), to name just a few. Early American quilters often traced around their kitchen utensils to make up their quilting designs of concentric circles, interlocking circles, waves, ropes, and vines. Almost any simple shape can be used— hands, feet, bird forms, flower forms, geometrics, some of those fantastic Art Nouveau shapes, symbols. Blow your grandmother's mind by quilting peace symbols all over a White House Steps quilt top. A Spirograph can be of great assistance in making your own designs, which can be transferred to the quilt's surface.

"Feather circle"

Some classic quilting patterns:

"Feather Garland"

"Twined Wave"

A compass and hand used as quilting patterns

The main consideration throughout this whole deal is to secure all three layers together so the stuffing doesn't shift; therefore, there shouldn't be wide expanses of space left on the quilt top when it is finished. Distances of not more than 2 or 3 inches of space are ideal if you are using a thin stuffing. Distances of 4 to 6 inches are acceptable for thicker stuffing.

As I mentioned, patchwork-patterned tops don't usually require very elaborate pattern considerations as the patchwork itself is the major quilting design. Appliqué patterns can pose very exciting challenges to the quilter as their patterns are usually very open, with lots of space. Theoretically, the back of the quilt should be as attractive as the top when the quilting is done. Keep this in mind when designing the quilting patterns you'll be using.

Draw full-size on newsprint paper the pattern or patterns you will be using. Trace them on tissue paper with a transfer pencil (found in good notion departments or needlecraft-supply houses) and press it out onto the quilt top. Or you can use a dressmaker's carbon and wheel—follow the directions for use on the package. Don't use typewriter carbon paper, it's not made for this purpose, and smears, and stains, and in general will spoil your disposition to quilt. You can use cardboard templates and trace your patterns with a sharp, hard-lead pencil. If you use this technique, be sure to sew on the pencil lines so they will disappear more readily. This technique is especially useful for repetitive patterns, as you'll only have to make the template once.

After you have put your quilting designs on the whole quilt top, using any one of the methods that you find most comfortable, you'll be ready to place the quilt into its frame for the actual quilting. If you are more existential by nature and wish to decide on pattern as you go along, you can do so right in the frames. This is especially effective for sampler quilts set in checkerboard fashion, with each patchwork or appliqué block containing a different pattern and alternating with blocks of solid colors with varying quilting designs.

Now can I quilt? Well ...

THE FRAME

You must build a quilting frame (actually there are other options open to you here; see page 49) and prepare the top, stuffing, and back for the frame, which takes longer to describe than to do. Some people have been able to buy an old frame for a few $$$ in country used-furniture stores, but you can easily construct your own with very little understanding of carpentry.   All you need are two 10-foot-long two-by-fours and one 8-foot-long two-by-four, a saw, a drill and 1/2-inch bit, 1/2-inch doweling, sandpaper, shellac or varnish, brush, staple gun, wide twill-tape (mattress ticking or heavy canvas strips will substitute nicely)—at least twenty feet of it—and four C-clamps (optional).   This will make a frame that is adjustable, large enough to carry a double-bed covering, and flexible enough to do smaller projects on.   Obviously, you'll need space to lay out your frame.   Don't panic, though, if you get a closed-in feeling with the prospect of a 10-by-4-foot frame; the directions can be modified to make a smaller frame if you need one.

Drill holes about 2 inches apart for about 2 feet through either end of each 10-foot length of two-by-four.   Saw the 8-foot two-by-four in half and drill holes 2 inches apart for 1 foot or so through either end of each half. Sand and smooth all the boards, smooth off the ends, and lay on a couple of coats of varnish or shellac.   Cut the doweling into 6-inch-long pegs, sand them smooth.   You'll need only four pegs at any time but cut yourself some extras anyway.   There's no need to shellac these.   You might have to sand them down a bit to fit.

Making a frame

If you can't find twill tape that is at least 4 inches wide dig up some canvas or ticking that wide. (Either get it from an upholsterer or make it yourself.) Fold the strips in half lengthwise and staple them to the 10-foot boards, keeping the fold away from the wood and skirting the holes. The frame is done.

To use the frame you'll need four ladder-back chairs you can prop the frame on, or two sawhorses 28 to 32 inches high, depending upon how tall you are and the height of the chair you'll be using. Your chair should be comfortable and armless so you can slide it under the frame. For me, the best frame height is a bit higher than elbow height when I sit in a chair. Finding the right chair and positioning of the frame should be done carefully. You'll be spending many hours here, and cricked backs and numb elbows can be avoided with a little thought. Many quilters prefer their frames chest high. They feel they can see the stitching better.

MOUNTING

The frame is ready for mounting the quilt. The fabric used for the back should be seamed together if necessary. The filling, which should be of the highest quality you can afford, can be purchased from most good department stores and fabric shops. Also, many craft and needlecraft magazines have advertisements with order forms for stuffing. It comes by the pound or in sheets folded and rolled. Cotton batting is most easily available, but some of the synthetics are rapidly gaining in popularity. They are light and easy to work with and produce a beautifully puffed product. By the sheet (synthetic or cotton) purchase double the yardage needed to cover the whole quilt, plus a few inches all around. One-half pound of cotton stuffing is needed per square yard of quilt to be covered. Check with the manufacturer to be sure. You can also use blanket flannel or an old woolen blanket as a filling if you don't need quite so much warmth and weight. Many old quilts had this kind of filling if the quilt was to be used in the summer or in warmer climates. This quilting is not as plush, obviously, but just as effective if done well.

If you are fortunate enough to have a carpet bigger than your quilt, or a floor you can push tacks into, great. If not, wide masking tape will do. Lay the backing with the fabric right side down on the floor. Pin, tack, or tape it to the floor with the sides parallel and the corners at right angles. Spread the filling over the backing evenly. If you are using sheets, lay them down in one direction, overlapping the edges about 1/4-inch, and then spread another layer on top of the first in the opposite direction, overlapping the edges as before. This prevents hollows showing through the top after quilting. The filling should extend beyond the backing's edges a bit.

Baste the filling to the back with long running stitches; start from the center and work out to the sides, then work from the center to the corners diagonally and all around the perimeter. Use a long needle and butt it against the floor as you baste so you know that you have stitched through both layers. Slide a piece of cardboard between the backing and carpet so you don't sew the two layers to the rug. A curved needle might help with the basting—bend one in a vice or look for a curved upholsterer's needle. Bladelike canvas needles can slash your backing, making it useless, so avoid them.

Iron the top again, smoothing all the wrinkles, and recheck to be sure that seams are all flat and to one side and all the corners are overcast. Be sure that all the surface basting stitches are removed. Lay the top down on the layers of backing and filling; it's sort of like one huge sandwich. All the sides should be parallel and coincide exactly with the backing; if not, there will be curling and sagging happening all over the place. Bad news. Trim the backing if it is too large for the top or vice versa. The corners should be at right angles to the sides. Use a protractor or a carpenter's right-angle. Baste the top down to the other layers, from the center out as before. Detach the whole thing from the floor. The entire surface should be smooth. The basting stitches should not be too tight or too small. The quilt stitching will actually secure the layers together; the basting is just to hold it together until it is mounted and sewn.

With the layers back on the floor, place the longest bars of the frame along the shortest ends of the quilt, facing the tape toward the quilt. Center the quilt on one of the bars by measuring and marking the center of the quilt's side and the center of the bar and matching the two. With the center marks together, stitch the quilt to the tape with even running stitches. Use strong thread (buttonhole twist or linen thread for braided rugs) and work from the center to each end. Repeat this procedure on the opposite side. The quilt must be centered or the surface of the quilt will be lopsided after you dismount it from the frame.

Mounting quilt on frame

With the help of a friend, roll the quilt under, carefully so that it is smooth and tight, an equal number of times on each bar. The top of the quilt is exposed. The two bars and rolled quilt should resemble the ancient scrolls of Jerusalem. The quilt is still on the floor. Slide the two shorter bars under the ends of the longer bars so that they are perpendicular to one another. <u>Carefully</u> unroll the quilt enough so that there are about 3 feet of quilt exposed between the bars. This is the area you will be quilting first. The center of the quilt should be in the center of the frame. Match holes in the bars and slip in a peg at all four corners. The corners must form right angles and the quilt must be suspended drum-tight between the bars; if not it should be rerolled. Again, the edges of the quilt and the blocks

44

must be at right angles. Check it all out now. This is the foundation for the quilting, and it must be done well or the resulting product will be disappointing. Lift the frame onto the four chairs or the sawhorses and prepare yourself for a new experience. For extra security use four C-clamps to hold the frame down to the horses or chairs.

NOW, you can quilt . . .

Frame mounted on horses
and quilt ready for stitching

QUILTING

Arm yourself with a pincushion liberally stabbed with sharp needles 1-1/2 to 2 inches long, an emery bag (usually the strawberry attached to a tomato pincushion) to sharpen your needles, a thimble if you can use one, otherwise a rubber filing tip (found in office-supply shops or stationery stores), or, if you are stubborn, develop a callus. A pair of sharp scissors, Band-aids for punctured fingers, some relaxing music, good light, your armless chair, and, last but not least, thread. White thread, standard mercerized sewing cotton #50, is good, though thread marked "quilting" is even better.

If you are ambidextrous you have been blessed with a quilter's most fond wish. If you are ambidextrous and very neat, so much the better. But if you are ambidextrous, neat, and <u>patient</u>, you have the whole thing licked. All of us can't be ambidextrous, but with a little effort we can develop neatness and patience, right? So my mother used to tell me.

Thread your needle with a double arm's-length of thread, knot both ends together, put on your thimble, and plunge ahead. With short, neat (there's that word again), even running stitches follow the lines of your quilting pattern from the center out. Punch your needle down at right angles to the surface, piercing all the layers, and then punch the needle back up through the layers almost at the point of entry. This gives a clean, fine line of stitches that won't shift any of the layers. Trace with the needle and thread along the edges of your patchwork or appliqué pattern about 1/16-inch from the seams. If the patch pieces or appliqué sections are large you may want to stitch a pattern within them.

The quilting stitch

Pull top and bottom layers together

Top
Filling
Bottom

Following the appliqué shapes as a quilting pattern

Quilting along pattern seams.

(Black thread is used for clarity in this illustration)

Finish quilting the exposed area between the bars. Detach the side bars and carefully roll the completed area up on one of the long bars, exposing a new area to be quilted unrolled from the other bar. Attach the bars together as before. Repeat this rolling and unrolling, moving from one side of the center to the other, until the quilting is finished. Through the whole process be sure everything remains smooth and tight and the corner angles are maintained always at right angles. While quilting, if you find that the surface becomes flaccid (lower in the middle than on the edges), lacing the edges of the exposed area you are working on to the side bars with strong white quilting thread or heavy linen rug thread will maintain the proper tension.

Lacing quilt to frame

When the quilting is complete, disassemble the frame and remove the quilt. Isn't it a beauty? Won't the Joneses next door just flip out? Prepare the binding for the edges, in a length that will go a few inches more than all around the perimeter of the quilt. Use bias strip binding prepared as described earlier, or commercial blanket binding, bias tape, or wide ribbon. Lay the quilt out on the floor and trim any excess filling. By hand or machine bind the edges, as shown.

Binding quilt edges

FANFARE, MUSIC, APPLAUSE (clap, clap, clap, clap, clap, clap, clap): your quilt is done.

Phew!

ALTERNATIVES:

Quilting can be done on a sewing machine; however, I use a machine only when the seams are so boringly straight and long that I can't bear the idea of stitching it all by hand. The thought of trying to work a large bed quilt under the needle of my machine without someone else to hold up the quilt's weight does not turn me on at all. I want quilting to be a creative, involving experience for the quilter, and the machine just puts itself between the person and the quilt. See what I mean?

If you are crammed into a small place or hassled about messing up the decor with a 10-by-4-foot frame complete with sawhorses, you can readily quilt each block separately and quite effectively on a quilting hoop. The quilting hoop is simply a glorified embroidery hoop. Of greater proportions than an embroidery hoop, it is used in much the same way—by stretching the area to be quilted over the hoop and stitching the layers of back, filling, and top the same as you would for the larger frame. Many quilters prefer the hoop to the large frame because it is more portable and can be left standing in a room without taking up all that space. You can either quilt each block upon completion of the patchwork or appliqué, and stitch the blocks together later, or you can quilt the entire top as already described.

You can also manufacture a much smaller frame with the inside measurements corresponding to the size of the blocks you plan to make. Just carve the directions down for the large frame to the desired size. A frame like this is good for smaller projects—clothing, hangings, and such—and is certainly more portable for people who keep on truckin'.

All the steps described earlier for mounting in the frame and quilting should be followed, with a few modifications. Most likely you will not have to roll your project up on the frame, but if you do it's exactly the same procedure as for the larger frame. If you want to quilt each block separately, baste the sandwich diagonally from corner to corner and all around the sides and proceed to mount it in the hoop or smaller frame and stitch. To connect the separate blocks together to make a complete quilt top, lay the blocks that go next to one another face to face and sew the tops together where the blocks join. Do this with long running stitches by hand or machine. Don't stitch through the filling or the back. Turn the blocks out and lay flat. Press the back edges under 1/4-inch and sew together, by hand, as shown. Be careful of your iron's temperature, especially if you are using a synthetic filling. When you have all the blocks sewn together in this manner you can quilt along the seams between each block: stretch the quilt in any one of the suggested frames and quilt-stitch about 1/4-inch away from the seam lines. You can also do this in your lap or on a table without

Pre-quilted block with
filling trimmed

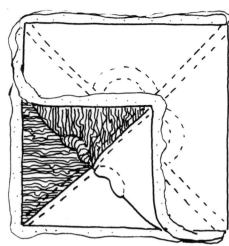

Two blocks face to face

Stitching with running stitch

edge folded under
¼ inch

Seaming back of blocks together

Joining the pre-quilted blocks

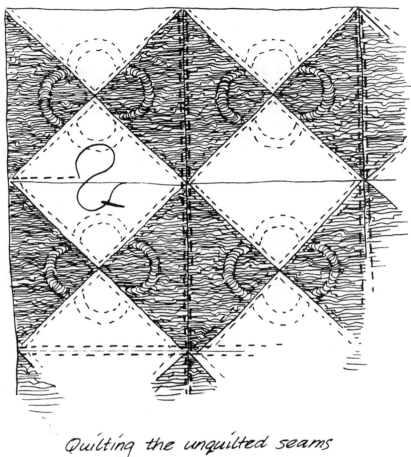

Quilting the unquilted seams

a frame, as it requires all straight stitching. A frame is necessary for fancier quilting. Bind the edges of your finished quilt top as already described.

If you are using a big frame and can't leave it set up in the middle of the room, prop it somewhere. Okay ... so your waterbed, Japanese screens, hookah, gas range, that old chest from the Salvation Army, your old man's easel, the parrot's cage, and your mother's snake plant are in the way, and you just can't bear to cover up Che's picture. Try the ceiling. Yeah, that's what I said. The ceiling. Attach eye screws from the hardware store to all the corners. If you can't do it yourself, have a friend who's into carpentry put a pulley system on the ceiling. With a set-up like that, all you have to do after a day's quilting is hoist it up to the ceiling. Fantastic for the acoustics.

Remember all the old cowboy movies when Gary Cooper would be a-courtin' his girl with fiddles and the dancing going on in the old ranch house? Everybody would be dressed to the nines, and a big feed was put up. Most likely this was a "bee" of some sort; nine times out of ten it would be a quilting bee. When a family had a few tops finished and ready for quilting they would throw a party that would last all day. Ten or fifteen needleworkers would start early and could finish a number of quilts by suppertime, working in shifts. It was a chance for an exchange of news and friendly conversation when casual visits would be impractical—distances and transportation time being what they were. Unlike canasta parties the bees would at least produce a usable product.

Think, if you had a quilt ready for quilting and had a few friends who knew how to stitch and you could manage to get them in the same place at the same time, you'd have a finished product in practically no time! In this day of social isolationism and super-mobility there is a need for tying people together, a chance to exchange views and relate to one another. The quilting bee is as good as any peace table, all parties working toward one goal in a mutual nonpolitical situation where generations can meet and talk. In our search for a road to the past and more peaceful days, or to a future where all people can work side by side happily, productively, and without hatred, as picayune an event as a quilting bee might also just put one more crack in the walls of despair and aloneness.

Carol

Sandalmaking

Betty Kusmin

There was a time when the fashion was to avoid facing feet. Feet were presumed to be the ugliest part of your body. As a kid I used to draw people standing in high grass so as to avoid having to capture that most difficult three-dimensional part of the standing figure. But the world turns and, ironically, I'm now a sandalmaker; and in the public sphere feet are in the spotlight. You now hear almost as many discussions about shoes and feet as you do about which car happens to be the safest and most economical. What kind of shoe is best for warmth? And which shoe offers the most freedom in summer?

In warm weather most of us are unhappy if we have to wear anything on our feet, and sandals provide the freedom of bare feet without any of the hazards or discomfort.

Custom-made sandals provide the most in the way of comfort and durability ... hand-wrought soles to protect your own natural ones. And some straps. No protection in themselves, it is interesting to remember that straps are there only to keep the foot on the sole. A string to tie the package.

These age-old devices are more similar to their ancient counterparts than any other single aspect of modern dress. In fact, all strap combinations are directly related to ancient strap design, which then, as now, was solely (sorry) concerned with simplicity, beauty, and comfort.

Custom sandals sell for $18 to $35 and even higher, and since to collect your supplies would cost about that, it is best to think in terms of learning a trade—making sandals for your family or community, on either a nonprofit or a professional basis. You certainly won't save much money just by making one pair for yourself. Handmade sandals are best, though, and are a good investment in the long run, for they can last fifteen years or more if they are resoled every few years. Improving with age, sandals take on the patina of old leather, and the markings from the toes become increasingly personal.

The time spent in learning sandalmaking is soon repaid because it's a craft there'll always be a demand for. A commercial sandalmaker friend used to scare beginners with lines like, "Go ahead and make your own sandals—get flat feet and stay out of the army." But that shouldn't deter; nobody gets flat feet from sandals, and the reality trip dictates that you take a look at a sandal and try to figure it out. And when you do, the mystery begins to evaporate quickly. Realizing that the straps and the top and bottom soles are the only major components, you'll see sandals can't be as complicated as some craftsmen make them out to be.

Most of us are a little awed by the craftsman's secrets. We're somewhat frightened of learning a new skill ourselves. This is even more the case when a craft is a functional one. If we attempt a leather wall-hanging and it's not quite right, that's o.k. We know we can alter it to suit our personal esthetic. We simply fiddle with it until it feels right, and in doing so we don't worry about whether we've weakened it structurally, etc. Even a handbag or belt, though utilitarian, doesn't have to fit a specific shape, like someone's foot. Knowing that sandals have to satisfy all the above needs, we become more concerned and anxious than we would with a wall-hanging. They have to fit and feel right.

Sandalmaking, then, only appears difficult because people usually fail to find out from sandalmakers the common sense behind much of the mystique. Practical underlying reasons for the process will become self-evident, for all the rules are there merely so the foot will be comfortable in the sandal. The beginner should be aware of certain things about sandals and feet before he begins. For starters, feet vary. Left foot differs from right foot. Walking habits vary. Leather has vagaries of its own, too, stretching and softening differently, according to tannage, climate, etc. All of this must be allowed for when you are constructing sandals. For instance, my own feet are flat and I need a sandal with more X-straps (to keep my foot anchored) than someone with good walking habits. A wearer with simple taste and good arches can manage fine with only two straps across the front, or else a simple T-strap, or a toe loop and arch strap.

TOOLS AND SUPPLIES

Leather suppliers should have everything you'll need for this new challenge. Look in the Yellow Pages for your area under Leather Suppliers. In Boston, The Berman Leather Co. and M. Siegel are two I deal with, and both Mr. Berman and Mr. Siegel are very helpful. In New York City I use A.C. Products. For good equipment, get the free catalogue from C.S. Osborne and Co., 125 Jersey St., Harrison, N.J. 97029. MacPherson Leathercraft Supplies, P.O. Box 395, San Francisco 94101, will send a free catalogue also. Tandy's is a chain of leathercraft shops located in Rochester, New York City, Albany, and who knows where else. This company offers a 10 percent discount if you purchase ten different items.

I let my leather supplier recommend what's best at the particular time I order. There are so many different names for grades and variations that I can't keep track of them all. Nor are the ones I want always in supply. Your supplier can really be a big help. Because he deals with other crafts-people and has the benefit of their combined experience and opinions, I have come to think of him as a headwaiter recommending the specialty of the day.

What you'll need:

SQUARE-EDGED LEATHER KNIFE: This is used to cut the soles out of the skin; it's also called a matte knife or four-way knife. Art-supply shops have this as well as hardware stores. It will cost 75¢ to $1.50.

2.

LIP KNIFE AND SLOT PUNCHES: The knife is for trimming. The punch will make the slot holes through which the straps run. Since both are expensive, confine yourself to just one 1/2-inch punch. If you're going to make a lot of sandals, then get all sizes of punches from 3/8-inch to 2 inches. The latter size is used for wide arch straps. A variety of punches enables you to make a large variety of sandal styles with different strap widths—a must for business.

3.   4.

PLOUGH GAUGE: This ensures a straight line when you cut straps, since it has a setting device to keep the width constant. If you are only doing a few pairs of sandals it doesn't pay to buy this tool. You can use a knife and steel ruler for cutting straps. But for a sandal business the plough gauge is indispensable.

this part of the plough gage
is a ruler

5.

BONDING CEMENT: With this you join bottom and top soles. A cement like Barges, gotten at craft shops, is very good. You'll need a glue brush to apply it. Since glue is not enough, by itself, to hold the sandals together, they'll also be cobbled (nailed together).

6.

TACK HAMMER, COBBLING NAILS, AND ANVIL: Nails should be brass and about 1/8-inch longer than the thickness of top and bottom soles. Nails are driven in through the bottom sole, and the anvil is used so the nail will bend back on itself and form a V when it hits the metal. Any steel object can replace the anvil if you're only making a few pairs of sandals.

7.

RAWHIDE MALLETS: These are useful for hitting and bonding the bottom and top soles together after they're joined by the glue (before nailing). Any wooden object for pounding, and wood to pound it on, will do, though, if you're only experimenting or not going into business.

8.

A <u>SKIVER</u> is a tool that holds and curves razor blades. This costs about a dollar and is used to thin (skive) the strap tips to feed through the sole hole and the tips of straps that go around the buckle. It is also used to skive the underside of both top soles where the straps cross under: by reducing the thickness, the sole will be flat, without lumps from the sandwiched straps. Don't skive out the bottom sole, as this will only decrease its life as it wears thinner. A matte knife can also be used to thin straps.

9.

<u>REVOLVING PUNCH</u>, for making the buckle hole. Since this runs about $15, skip buying it and have a shoemaker put the buckle on for you.

10.

<u>RIVET SETTER</u>: A shoemaker can also eliminate the necessity of buying this item, which is used for attaching rivets in buckle placement. Again, when you do a lot of sandals this tool will come in handy. You can avoid the need for the setter, however, by making sandals with ties, or the kind that are of the permanent nonbuckle variety.

11.

SANDPAPER: In finishing, the edges of the sandals must be ground smooth by using <u>coarse</u> sandpaper wrapped around a block. Then use <u>fine</u> sandpaper for continued sanding. Next, buff the edges with a soft rag or lambswool. For making sandals commercially, you'd best buy a motorized sander with interchangeable discs.

12.

13. Using a motorized sander

Sandals needn't be dyed, the oil from feet helps darken them naturally. Personally I prefer this look. For commercial production, however, it's best to have some aniline dyes handy. Most customers want their sandals dark when purchased, and customer education in this matter is more arduous than dyeing the sandals. Fiebing's Leather Dye shines up well and costs, at most, only 75¢. Use it on the edges of soles and straps.

14.

For finishing and preserving the sandals, use leather oil. Hardware stores, as well as leather suppliers, will have in stock Neatsfoot Oil and/ or Lexal. By accident, I once drank some Lexal. It looks like stale coffee, and I was in the habit of storing it in a paper cup. When phoned, poison control informed me it was nontoxic. Nevertheless, I don't recommend it for coffee breaks. Come to think of it—it might be a good idea to label your liquid supplies. Tell the wearer to continue to use this oil when the sandals have gotten wet. Puddles and rain cause leather to lose its natural oils, and eventually it becomes brittle unless treated with preservative oils as a safeguard.

THE SKIN TRADE

Buying leather isn't all that difficult, even though there's a mystique attached to it. Sandalmakers can be overheard talking about the relative merits of chrome versus oak tannage, etc., etc. Since only oak-tanned leather can be molded into an arch, I always use a 12-ounce (or so) oak-tanned bend cowhide for the bottom sole and an 8-ounce shoulder cowhide for the top. Bend cowhide is from the back and rump of the animal, and large bend skins are available. Shoulder cowhide is not as strong. That is why it is advisable to use it only for the top sole. See your leather supplier for advice on different sole tannages.

I definitely prefer thick to thin bottom soles—not just for impressing customers or even for durability, although these are advantages, but because a thick sole acts better as a cushion against hard surfaces and sidewalks, and therefore is a good preventer of foot fatigue. (Somebody may want a thinner bottom sole, so a commercial sandalmaker would be wise to keep some around. Just in case.)

For straps I like horsehide. But since it can't always be gotten I use latigo (another tannage leather) for adjustable sandals. Latigo comes in some lovely colors and also takes a stain beautifully. But it has too much stretch for a fixed-strap sandal (this is one whose straps are attached permanently, with no buckle or tie for adjustment).

I find it pays to use the best leather available regardless of price because the difference in cost between fine and mediocre leather per pair never seems to exceed a couple of dollars, and in retailing this difference is readily and profitably absorbed.

Built-in obsolescence doesn't work in this craft. Generally, the longer a pair of sandals lasts, the more a customer should want to buy. He will feel more like a collector of various styles and less like a sucker forced to repeat his mistake. Discerning and appreciative people like custom-made sandals, and this is one of the major rewards that come from working in this particular craft field.

THE PATTERN

Both feet are outlined while the person you're making the sandals for stands on a piece of paper, feet slightly apart, weight evenly divided. It gets embarrassing rummaging around tearing apart old lunch bags. Mayonnaise twixt the toes is a drag. So have lots of oak tag handy. This is a lightweight board about as cheap as anything you'll find—about 7¢ a sheet. When tracing, hold the ballpoint pen or pencil vertically in order to get a true outline. The space between the first and second toes should be marked for the toe thongs. The arch is marked in depth by sliding the pen under the foot; both the length and highest point of the arch should be indicated. This will help in molding the bottom sole. Do this accurately!

15.

There are four main bones you want to mark when fitting the sandal. These bones should be paid special attention to because straps <u>must not</u> go over the bones.

16.

Once the foot is outlined, draw an evened-out contour of the tracing about 1/4 inch outside the original drawing. This contour is, natch, the sandal pattern. I leave a bit more than 1/4 inch around the toes (toes spread after a bit of exposure to sandals). You need a margin for error mostly around the toes and also somewhat at the heel. This allows for changes in walking habits. Later, after the sandals have been worn for a while, any excess can be ground off. (I believe in lots of fail-safes.) You can create pleasing shapes for what may be a rather strange foot. Also, you can make these contours the same for the right and left feet, even though the actual contour differs. The outside line in the drawing of the sandal sole below is the outer edge of the top sole. The inner line (or exact contour) shows you where to place the straps. Here is one example of possible strap placement.

17.

The strap marks go <u>slightly on the inside</u> of the inside line so the straps will come into the sandal <u>under the foot</u>. Place straps <u>only</u> where there are no bone markings, since a strap will chafe and hurt if it rubs on the bone. You can punch slots in the tracing and weave the straps through to see if they look right. (More details on strap placement when we discuss different sandal styles.)

Once the straps are marked, put the pattern on the top-sole leather and cut flush with the outside contour of the pattern. Then punch the slots where they're marked for straps. Be careful, for this is a crucial part of the operation. Sometimes you'll perhaps punch those slots too far in. In this case don't use the leather for that particular sandal. But save that top sole! It can be pared down for a smaller size or else used as a sample in your sandal business.

If the slots are in the right place, everything else will follow smoothly and you'll have a well-fitting sandal. But even a slight error in slot placement will cause a poor fit. If you're unsure, seek some advice before proceeding with this operation. A look at the illustration below may help clarify things for you, however.

18.

The next step involves the cutting of the bottom soles. Cut them out of your leather 1/2 inch to 1 inch larger (all around) than the top soles. This allows for shrinkage in the next procedure, which entails molding the bottom soles to the foot. This is done after the bottom soles have been soaked in water for a half-hour or so and then left to partially dry for a few hours. (Too much soaking and the leather flops back to its original flatness.)

19.

After your bottom sole has lost much of its moistness, hold it to the foot and mold a fairly exaggerated arch, with a corresponding cupping or raised edge around the toe and heel. This will look extreme at first, but will soon sag into a more realistic shape. Arches always mold more easily to the wearer's foot if they start out too high rather than too low. If the arch is drastically high, just sit on it for awhile for a quick collapse.

The bottom sole will have to dry thoroughly before you glue it to the top sole, so allow several days for complete drying. Cloudy, damp days make for even slower drying, but you can speed things up a bit with a fan. This molding process is one of the main reasons for the notorious slowness of sandalmakers. There is one perfectly acceptable shortcut around this lengthy waiting, however, for professionals; a number of bottom soles can be uniformly cut and molded in a very large pattern. This premolding process underlines my belief that individually molded arches are not as important as many buyers and sandalmakers have come to believe. In actuality, the foot molds the arch, so the only drawback to this faster method is the waste when you strip off excess bottom-sole leather to fit the customer's foot. But it is a good approach to solving the problem of impatient buyers. This trimming is where your lip knife proves most helpful.

Instead of molding the heel, you can make a small heel for your sandal. This heel is merely the shape of the heel of the bottom sole, glued and cobbled onto the bottom sole. It can be replaced when it wears down, for it is the first place to show real signs of wear.

STYLES

Both fixed and adjustable straps keep the foot on the sole. With the fixed-strap style, the strap that prevents the foot from moving forward off the sole is the toe thong or toe loop. These go between the first and second toe or over the big toe and prevent the foot from moving forward. Some people find these loops irritating and uncomfortable at first, but it usually only takes a day or two to break in the sandal. Sometimes I use a clothespin to pinch that part of the leather thong that goes between the two toes. This helps speed up the breaking-in process.

20.

An alternative barrier to the foot moving forward is a strap across the foot just behind the two front bones. The bones and straps keep each other in place. To keep the foot from sliding backward you'll place a strap that ties or buckles high around the heel. Unless you have long straps tied up the leg, gladiator style, you'll need side tabs to keep the heel strap high. To keep the foot from sliding sideways use either an arch strap (Fig. 22) or an X strap (Fig. 23). Both of these come across the instep of the foot.

21.

23.

22.

These are the basic straps, and all variations in sandal style come from combinations of them. You can experiment by winding straps around your own feet until you come up with something pleasing that works. The number of possible designs is endless, but keep in mind they must all work for the structural purpose intended: to keep the sole on the foot comfortably and gracefully.

24.

Remember, no straps should feed into the sandal over a bone, or the wearer will be uncomfortable. The bones are useful as tension points, with the straps either in front of or behind them, depending on the way the strap functions. That is why bones should be marked carefully in the first place, and those marks considered when the slot marks are placed. Most sandal discomfort comes from carelessness in this aspect of sandalmaking.

Next, skive the flesh (under) side of the top soles where the straps lie. Some straps will loop under the top sole from one slot to another. This area, too, will need to be skived. For permanent straps, skive about 1 to 1-1/2 inches from the slot, or turn them toward the outside edges and don't skive at all.

25.

GETTING IT ALL TOGETHER

Now that the bottom sole is molded and the top sole is punched, cut the straps. As I say, horsehide makes for very nice straps, but, if unavailable, use latigo. Now you put that four-way knife and steel ruler or the plough gauge to use. To attach, feed straps through slots in the top sole.

26.

If yours is a fixed-strap sandal, you'll first glue the straps down to the underside of the top sole after having achieved the required tightness (at a fitting) on the wearer's foot: when the foot slips in and out of the sandal with <u>slight</u> difficulty. Straps stretch. So don't worry about overtightness as long as the sandal can be gotten on and off. There is an alternative to gluing: you can turn one end of each fixed strap toward the center, and the other end toward the outside. This makes it easier to tighten later if the straps stretch. You'll be able to tighten without opening up the entire sandal. Both methods have their advantages, and fine sandalmakers practice each method. If yours is an adjustable style, simply weave the long single strap through the top sole but do not glue it. And be careful not to glue this strap when gluing top and bottom soles together. You want it to remain free. When gluing, be sure to follow specific instructions on your cement can.

Glue the underside of the top sole.

Join it to the glued underside of the bottom sole.

27.

Now glue top sole to bottom sole and give it a once-over, all-over hammering job.

28. Hammer the glued-together top and bottom soles while the glue is still tacky

After the glue has dried, the next step is cobbling (nailing) around the entire edge of the sandal. This furthers the work of the glue and helps keep the sandal from coming apart. Place nails about 1 inch apart, and in from the edge about 1/4 inch. Remember to hammer against an anvil or metal object so the nail turns back on itself. (By the way, you're working the nails in alternately from the bottom and the top of the sole, for strength.) Be careful not to drive the nails through the adjustable straps, or, naturally, they won't adjust. Making small holes first helps when you're pounding in the nails.

29.

Cobbling the arch helps it stay up longer. Drive the nails in perpendicular to the arch; this involves tilting the sandal on the anvil to get the angle right. About ten nails in the arch should be ample.

30.

Mention should be made here of an alternate method of bonding the top to the bottom sole—stitching. It is a process that is seldom used, for it is time-consuming, and only if applied with much exactitude is it as efficient and attractive as the cobbling technique.

TRIMMING, DYEING, AND FINISHING

If the edges are cut carefully there won't be much hassle in the trimming of them. After trimming go around the edges with rough and then fine sandpaper (as described under Supplies). Finally, buff with any soft cloth or lambswool.

Buckles get put on last. Remember! Heelstrap buckles fall on the outside of each foot in front of the heel, <u>not</u> on the bone. The buckle is attached by rivets to the strap that comes from the front outside of the sandal. Punch holes for closing the buckle on the other straps. Allow for stretch by providing lots of extra holes, about 1/2 inch apart. Either have this done by a shoemaker, or, if you've obtained the somewhat costly (around $6) rivet setter, follow the instructions that come with it for attachment of the buckle.

31.

Any dye, if desired, is now applied. The sandal gets oiled, rubbed, and hand-polished, and is then ready for wear.

Happy walking!

Betty Kusmin

Woodblock Prints

CARDBOARD CUT

PASTE-ON CARDBOARD CUTOUT

MULTIBLOCK COLOR PRINTS

ONE-BLOCK WATERCOLOR WOODCUT

Jean Young

Woodblock is historically the earliest method of printing designs on paper and textiles. When ink is applied to one side of a block of wood, and paper is pressed onto the block, the ink is transferred to paper. I was soaking in the tub one day, thinking about how to describe the printing process, when it finally hit me that the water was cold. I climbed out shivering and jumped all over the bath mat and bathroom floor to warm up, and there they were... a dozen or more examples of the printing method! Lots and lots of footprints. The whole scene down there looked like an Escher woodblock, with unfallen arches all over the place looking like some kind of solar primeval dance had gone down. There was one difference, which took me half an hour to figure out. The wet foot is placed on the bath mat, and in woodblock, paper is placed on the wet block, and then it's turned over when you go to see the print. This means the print is in reverse from the way you executed it on the block—the left side will be on the right side and the right side on the left. If conceiving your design in reverse is going to create a mental block right away, there are ways to get around this, so don't cop out.

The Chinese, who discovered this process, used it to print the written characters of their language. They found that when they hollowed out a shape in the wood, the raised part, when inked black, would be the only part to print.

If thinnish lines are cut away from the block, black ink is rolled over the surface with a roller, and paper is pressed on the block, the lines will not print, and the image will be like a white line drawing on black.

White-line woodblock: Ajax (1932)

74

You can transfer a drawing to tracing paper and then to the block by turning it over (in reverse of the original), and, with carbon paper next to the woodblock, redrawing it. A carbon copy appears on the block. You also can use a pencil on the block as your beginning point; or you can start right off gouging out your design. (More later about tools.) Sensibility comes through direct this way. It also provides that immediacy for people who don't like to plan ahead, and the excitement that comes from the unexpected.

White lines are the easiest and most natural to the block-print medium. Integrated white and black lines can make the most of the woodblock technique. However, if fewer black lines and more white lines are used, the actual work will be easier than the other way around.

Woodblock by an early Provincetown printmaker (1916). Here white lines are preferred over black.

When a black line is wanted instead of a white line, you have to go to much more trouble. Draw on the block where you want it to print black, and then cut away all the surface around the line you want to print. When inked, the print will come out looking much like your original drawing on the block, dark lines on white paper.

Black-line woodblock:
A Medieval Herb Garden (16th century)

In the fifteenth century the dark line was preferred over the white line by European artists. Had preparing black-line woodblocks been a simple, rapid, and natural process, artists would have continued to make their own designs, cut their own blocks, and do their own printing. Imagine how much more time would have to be spent cutting a block if you wanted to make a fish-net pattern of black lines and the background white, instead of composing the picture so that the net could be of white lines and the space around them black. The more tedious woodblocking became, the more the artist did only the original drawing; a craftsman transferred it to the block and cut it, and a third person did the printing.

During most of the nineteenth century the poor woodblock had no real character of its own because everyone insisted that it must look like something else—drawings, etchings, charcoal drawings, washes, or even photographs. One medium imitating another is a sort of never-ending round robin, and the results are hypocritical because they pretend to be something they aren't. An emphasis on technique will cause the material you use to lose its identity. Anyone who gets to know woodblock, and loves it for what it is, will prefer those prints that remain true to the character of woodblock, and you'll notice they have more vitality, too. A lot of work by M.C. Escher is woodblock.

The idea you want to express is always preeminent, and craft secondary. Learning the craft is the easiest part of the trip. And there are many things you can find woodblock useful for: posters, decoration for catalogues, a total design for newspaper ads, birth announcements, greeting cards of all sorts, and wrapping-paper design; you can also print your own wallpaper using oil inks or acrylic paint.

ENVIRONMENT

It takes a while to build up to the level of being strung out on your own work. Start by concentrating on your working environment, which will help you get off. Eventually, you will have accumulated so many images and ideas you'll want to make into prints, you'll have no problem beginning. Your ideas will expand so much that the constant build-up creates a need to get them out of your system by getting them down on paper.

When you're beginning, and even later on, it's nice to go to a little trouble to settle in properly in a working area. Some burn incense, but a must is burning lights if it's not bright enough. Light is so good for the eyes. Some years ago, when I was material for the martyr-stoic syndrome, I thought a hard chair was good for hard thinking, but I've had to face the fact that I feel interrupted if it's too cold or too hot or a chair too hard or too low for working. Now I really notice it if it's too stuffy and odors from turpentine and paint fill the air or if my environment is too quiet. I like to hear human activity around. It makes me feel less uptight and more integrated with the world. The ivory tower is too remote and one can get twisted up there and trapped in a time warp, with only the reality of the sound of your own tools working the wood. Feel into it. Ask yourself what makes you more comfortable and free, and take some time out to put it together.

TOOLS AND SUPPLIES

MATERIAL FOR CREATIVE ENERGY: All I've ever needed, or gotten the habit of needing, are candy and coffee while working. They energize me and intensify my ability to zero in and get what I want done. Once I get into a project, I get stoned on the experience of doing it and forget the candy. Dylan Thomas was a candy-bar freak, too.

The worst part of being a sweet freak is that too much candy can be a real bummer. Sometimes I've really gone too far and sort of O. D. 'd on it. After a lot of bad anxiety about too much candy and too much coffee, I finally talked myself into modifying the whole creative energy consumption habit. Five years ago I was smoking too, and what with turpentine from all the oil painting I was doing, I was living at a near-toxic level. If you're a health freak, and you should be, try Fig Newtons and juices.

Music can also be a way to start the creative energy flowing. If you're a purist, listen to Mozart before you start your work. It is better for clearing your head than sweeping the back porch like some Zen monks do before they start their creative work. Mozart doesn't just leave you empty but full of vibrations moving out of pure clarity. Sometimes I work with a James Brown record on in the background, especially at night. The natural free wild energy and directness will keep you company, but you've got to cool it if you leave your work table dancing and exhaust your energy.

GOUGES AND CUTTING KNIFE: Woodblocks can be cut with one good knife. The bigger art-supply stores sell very good woodcutting knives and gouges singly. Try to buy the best, which would be of well-tempered steel. Small art shops will only carry sets of six, which run between $8 and $15. These include the cutting knife and gouging tools in V- and U-type shapes, and also a chisel to shave out larger areas of wood. Tools get dull fast cutting wood, and a sharpening stone is a necessary item (available at both art-supply and hardware stores, and relatively expensive—around $2). For

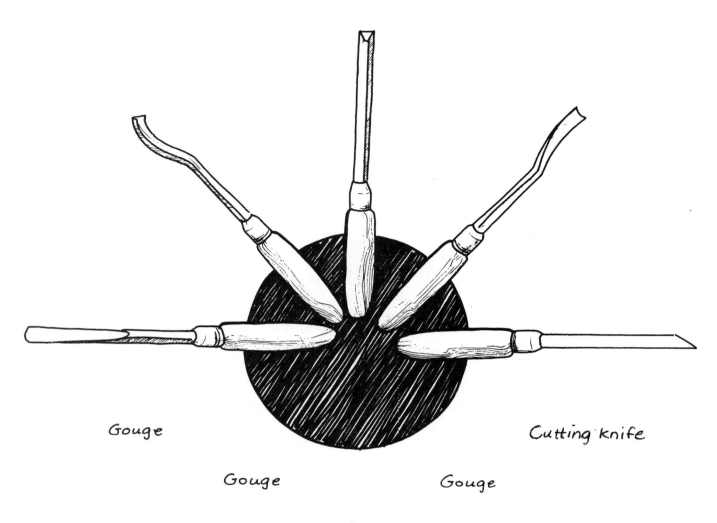

Gouge

Gouge   Gouge

Cutting knife

Chisel

this reason, I don't recommend getting the cheap Japanese set of twelve carving tools, which are only $2 or so. They will dull right away and won't take a new edge. Some people just use a pocket knife and find that's all they need. In any case, getting initial supplies should be the least of your worries because none will cost you any heavy bread.

If you are starting to cut for the first time, don't chew a Butterfinger because the name might have more power of suggestion than creative energy and you'll end up with a finger that looks like a Tootsie Roll.

PAPER: Try anything that is somewhat absorbent (most paper is absorbent if it is thinnish). A light cream newsprint paper is perfect, and people use it for pulling their first prints. One of the reasons newsprint is not used other than in the trial printing is that it can ruin your whole act because it doesn't stand up over the years, and anything you want to save for more than two years can't be counted on remaining in good condition.

Rice paper is the best and comes in sheets and pads at the art shops. Sheets can be cut to size for your block, but a smart way to buy is to remember the size of your block if you have one, and buy sheets or pads that will be 2 or 3 inches larger all the way around than your block. Most rice paper is white, but if you find a cream paper and use it, your print will have a richer effect.

Heavy paper, even if it looks absorbent, will not grab all the ink off the block as easily as the thinner paper. Another advantage of thinnish paper is that the ink or at least a clear impression comes through the back of the paper, so it is easy for you to see what you're doing when rubbing the ink onto the paper.

When using a water-base ink or watercolor paint, and if you want a softer edge to the shapes and lines on your print, heavier paper can be dipped in water, pressed between sheets of newspaper, and then used in dampened condition. Good lithograph paper is beautiful, substantial, and soft, and if you can find a way to use it in woodblock, so much the better. Use any color paper you want, but mostly you'll find white or cream.

THE WOOD: There are many nice things happening at the lumber yard. It's a world of big space devoted to a big natural resource. The smells of pine and cedar, the not altogether unpleasant sounds of the power tools, and the preoccupied shouts of the carpenters and workmen drown out your connection with the outside world. The fact that you are there with apparently wanton abandon, compared to those zapped heads paying heavy lumber bills and crazed goons taking away tons of lumber for more Levittowns, enables you to really enjoy the whole scene.

A relatively big section of the Woodstock Lumber Yard is for storage of the end pieces remaining from ordered-to-size jobs. It usually takes me a long time to adjust to so many choices. No one bothers me and I take my time. Just hanging around and getting familiar with the place has improved my attitude towards building. I'm not afraid of a table saw and have used it a lot for picture-framing and remodeling our farmhouse. There's nothing to cutting and cracking sheet-rock, and anyone can hammer.

I usually end up taking more pieces of wood for woodblock home with me than I need, and the lumber yard used to give them away. The relative freedom in picking these blocks up and getting into their various surfaces and feel started me out painting on wood. They've been charging for wood the last few years, but the cost is so little that you can count on this being the cheapest part of the craft supply.

Any size block can be used, as long as the paper you have will be more than enough to cover it. A convenient size is about 10 inches by 14 inches, and look for pieces that are at least 3/4 to 1 inch thick. This will help guarantee that the plank will be absolutely flat with no warpage—check this out before selecting. Also find pieces that have at least one side free of any knots. Ink will not adhere well to knots. If you find wood free of knots on both sides, you can use both sides for cutting. The best way is to know your paper size beforehand, and find a size (or else have a piece cut down to size) to fit the paper.

Any wood, providing it isn't too hard or too soft, can be used. Pine boards (soft wood) are good. Of course, if you can get ahold of pear wood, like Escher did, try that. And, if you feel like experimenting, try pieces that have been crosscut out of a small tree and sand them down.

INKS: Art shops sell block-printing inks for about 60¢ a tube. These come in either oil or water base. Water-base prints are matte (that is, the ink has a flat, dullish surface) and they dry faster, so you usually don't need to rig up something to hang these prints to dry on. Oil-base ink is thinned down with turpentine. There is also an extender available to give you more mileage. Oil-base has a slickish surface and will take a while to really dry, so these prints must be hung up in a clothesline situation with either clothespins or the Bulldog paperclips that dime stores and art shops carry.

The basic trouble with the lines of printing ink generally available in retail shops is that the choice of colors is too limited and they don't mix well. People who do color printing for the most part use the multiblock method (described later) and need a limited color selection in the first place—that's why manufacturers of the ink feel they don't have to provide a good range of colors.

When doing the one-block print, where you cover the entire block with one color, I suggest using black. Then your two colors will be black and white (if you use white paper). This still remains the color scheme most natural to woodblock printing. But I don't want you to be stuck on any theories! Matisse's collages of large sitting figures look great in the color he chose—a sky-blue placed on white paper—so you will want to psych out any color that will suit your purpose.

ROLLERS: These are called brayers in art-supply stores. They will run between $1.50 and $6. The most expensive is also the best because it is softer. An adequate brayer runs about $3. The cheaper ones are too hard: wood inside, a thin cover of rubber on the outside.

Brayer

PALETTE: Thick glass (or thin glass with a few layers of newspaper under it) is the best possible palette on which to roll the brayer in the ink, and the best possible thing for mixing all kinds of paint. Painting the underside of the glass with white paint makes a perfect white surface for seeing colors clearly. Placing the glass on top of white paper will also do the trick. Soft or hard paint and ink can all be easily scraped off glass with a single-edge razor blade. If the edges of the glass are too sharp, a quickie solution is to run some Scotch tape along them; however, paint will eventually get stuck on the tape.

DOING IT

CUTTING THE BLOCK: This is a woodchopper's ball, and one part of the whole process is to SEE what you're doing. If you're wearing dark glasses, take the lenses out first. The block should be cut with the knife blade slanting toward the middle of the cuts, forming a V. Slanting the knife toward the side of the cut will make an undercut, weakening the raised edge, which may eventually chip off. The knife is used for cutting out white lines, for cutting outlines of areas that will later be completely gouged and chiseled away, and for cutting outlines around lines that will stay raised and print black. Hold gouges so that the handle is up against the palm of your hand for maximum pushing pressure. Your fingers guide the cut. It is important, right off, to get into the habit of working the gouge away from you, away from the hand steadying the block. If not, as you push the gouge it could slip off the block, cutting or jabbing your other hand. If you're a strung-out neurotic or nervous type, don't listen to hard rock or you might end up with a cut Tootsie Roll. Just make do with a little light, lobotomized music, as long as it's good stuff. Nailing a strip of wood onto your working table and placing the edge of the woodblock against that while working on it will keep the block, but not the gouge, from slipping. (Large areas of wood can be chiseled away.)

Cut into the wood at a depth that comes natural to what you're cutting, at least 1/16-inch deep as a rule. But narrow spaces are cut shallower than the wider ones. If a largish space is cut too shallow, it will be hard to keep the ink out of it when you roll ink on the block, and then it will print when the paper is laid down.

This is where you can work out any latent hostility. It is also the time to eat a Mars Bar. You are really attacking, and unless you want to cop back into the system, this part of the process is a good exercise in going against the grain.

Picasso said once that he destroyed in order to create. He would wipe out his own efforts to get something better. He also liked to work in a messy, cluttered room; it made him feel like creating order out of all the chaos.

Don't get me wrong, all this aggression shouldn't spill over into your philosophy of life, or influence your attitude about people—not like the ego-mongers' power-trip on the political machine that destroys in war, they tell us, in order to "create peace" and "make the world safe." In cutting the block you are putting human energy into the wood as you destroy it. Your energy in man/woman-made forms and structures can say what you want it to say through the impression of the wood pressed into your print. Nothing lost—everything ingrained.

PRINTING: When you are ready to print, bite off a chunk of Heath Bar and roll the brayer over the ink on the glass palette so it spreads even all along the brayer. Roll the ink on the block, then place a sheet of your printing paper on top of the inked block. Hold one hand down on the paper while rubbing sections of the surface with the back of a tablespoon until the entire surface has been burnished. Hold the spoon so that your thumb presses down in the center of the spoon. This is the part of the process that really uses some energy. (That's another advantage of eating candy now and then.) A clean brayer can be used and also a low-heated iron, and you can even stomp'n'rock on it, but nothing is as good as the spoon to burnish the paper so you won't lose consistency of pressure in all areas. A silver spoon, if kept polished, is best.

Roll the ink on the block

Burnishing with a spoon.

Finished prints will take a while to dry and should not be stacked on top of each other. If you do a few prints, you'll no doubt have enough floor and table space to lay them down on. But remember, oil inks take longer to dry than water-base inks, and you may need to hang oil prints.

THE CARDBOARD PRINT

There are two ways to use cardboard for printing. Both are perfect, since they can be done quickly and, also, much experimentation can take place. (1) Shapes can be cut out of cardboard with scissors or knife with little hassle and arranged and glued onto a stiff surface;

(2) Cuts can be made in thick cardboard in the same manner as in wood.

MATBOARD: Single-thick costs around $1 for a sheet 30 inches by 40 inches and runs about half that price in the 20 by 30 size, at any art-supply shop. Generally, just small pieces of matboard will serve your purpose because you will be cutting out forms to glue onto a large surface. Since matboard is generally used to mat pictures for framing, perhaps you can get pieces (for free or for very little money) that the framer has cut out of the center of his mats. This way, you might get different textures to experiment with. Pebbleboard is speckled with little holes. A friend likes to put even more holes in pebbleboard with an ice pick.

Double-thick matboard is about double the cost of the single-thick, but it's necessary if you want to cut into it, as in the woodblock method. Little texture will come through on your print when you use cardboard and it is less expensive than matboard or wood. (Grayboard is cheaper but not so many shops stock it.)

A UTILITY KNIFE is best for cutting into cardboard or matboard. Blades can be replaced when they wear out. The cost is about $1 per knife, and they can be gotten at hardware and art stores. (It's also called a mat knife.)

PAPER: Same as used in woodblock; thinnish paper is best (for grabbing all the ink) especially in cardboard printing.

DOING IT AS IN WOODBLOCK: Using a double-or triple-thick matboard or cardboard, make line cuts about 1/16-inch deep into the cardboard with the mat knife. Use the mat knife to outline any areas that are to be cut away. Then use the mat knife to pick into the cut and lift up the areas and peel them away (cardboard is composed of layers of paper).

When the cut is finished and ready to print, you must shellac the surface (even the cuts). Any other kinds of medium might dissolve oil or water inks, so be careful what you use. Polymer Medium, which you use with acrylic paints, might work, as might Sobo or Elmer's Glue, if you have any around the house. Although these are water-base, when they dry they won't be dissolved by either oil or water-base ink or paint. But varnish, for instance, will dissolve oil. Shellac brushed on is best for your health, unless it comes in spray cans. Who needs more toxic material in their body? Spray outside and get it done quickly, if you do spray.

If you need sugar-induced creative energy and drink coffee, more poison will matte your mind and fuzz you down. By the way, I've found that a good way to face up to commercial candy products is to chomp a chunk off your favorite bar and just let it float around in your mouth and melt; then analyze what it really tastes like. If your taste is like mine, it will taste like a lot of cheap chemicals. This is a moment for revelation.

DOING IT BY GLUING: In this method complete shapes are cut out of single-thick cardboard or matboard and glued onto masonite, plywood, or any other kind of stiff surface. This surface can be painted white so that its color won't interfere with your color design. Those who have done collage (pasting paper on paper) will like this number because the principle is the same. Cutting with scissors is easiest. The cut-out pieces can be arranged on the base surface with experimentation and spontaneity, balancing the forms, shifting them around, taking pieces out, putting another shape in, until you have them in positions you want to make permanent. Even then, when they are glued down, you can cut parts of your design away with the utility knife, then sandpaper the surface; you can always add to it, and cut in lines as in woodblock.

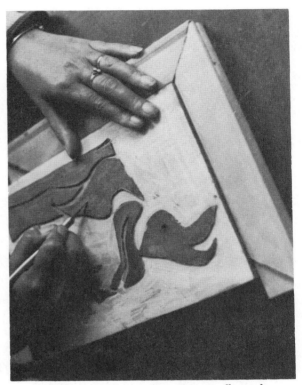

Cutting in lines after the cardboard pieces have been glued down

In doing abstractions, if you feel your arrangement or organization looks like the kiss of death—dried up and dull—just to show yourself what a totally uninhibited arrangement would look like, try throwing the pieces on the block and see how they fall. Also, try putting some pieces in reverse or upside down. There is great value in seeing what an accident or inverted thinking will do. If you want to print a trial run to see clearly how it will look when it is reversed, or if you're not sure you will like the arrangement tomorrow, glue it all down with rubber cement (which is a temporary glue), shellac, and print as a test. When you want the pieces to be glued permanently, use Sobo or Elmer's. It helps to place a heavy book on top of the permanently glued parts for half an hour.

Jim Forsberg, who discovered this cardboard method (when he came out of the Army in 1946), told me an easy trick. If you have a hard time thinking and working in reverse, arrange your cut-out forms on the size block you want, Sobo the <u>top</u> of the cardboard pieces, then place another block (any surface the same size) on top of the glued pieces. When you turn the block around, the pieces will be in reverse and glued in place. When you print onto the printing paper and turn the paper around, it will be like your original arrangement. Shellac and print.

With this kind of printing, edges have a softer quality than woodblock.

Another thing Jim discovered was that some people did not like the print cut away from the edges of the paper. (Collectors buying Japanese prints, for instance, are very careful to see that the original edge of the paper is intact on a print they want.) Because of this, he had to be careful and line the paper straight with the block because he couldn't trim down any off-center edges. Center by measuring with a ruler. Or, if you can, do it by eye—when you find the corners of the block under the paper, press with your fingers. Since Jim was arranging roundish shapes (to express his feelings about seeing Stonehenge when he was in the Army) by isolating them in space, he had no edge to his picture, so he inked the edges of the block and printed. That gave him the boundary he needed and at the same time saved the original paper edges.

COLOR PRINTING—MULTIPLE BLOCKS

What I'm most interested in is the one-block watercolor method of wood-cutting, but I will explain first how color is printed in the traditional way—the Chinese and Japanese method. It is time-consuming and limits the color you use, but after a lot of work cutting several blocks, you do have the advantage of being able to print, say, 100 prints relatively quickly.

Each color must be printed from an individual block: five colors, five blocks. This is such a drag. A two- or three-color print is a fair challenge, but using ten or more colors gets tedious. (Naturally, there is no limit, except the limit to your patience.) This process takes so long that in the traditional Japanese printing process, there was a three-man team involved—the artist who drew the design, the woodblock cutter, and finally the printer.

For this technique, you need a registration board so each printing will go exactly where it should. If two colors overlap (where they shouldn't), the registration is off. It isn't a big deal to make a registration board. Three-quarter-inch plywood or shelving (unwarped), larger than your paper size, will be the base. Consider the largest size you might be working on in the future so you won't have to make another one. Next nail a strip of wood (1 to 2 inches wide) and almost as thick as the woodblock along both the top edge of the board and the left side. This forms a right angle that your woodblocks can be put up against.

From under the top strip, run two long finishing nails through both base and strip so that the points will protrude a few inches at the top. Printing paper will be registered correctly when the same sheet of paper is placed at different times for different colors through the same nail holes.

Registration board

Now cut a key block (the complete picture). It is placed on the registration board snug up against the right angle. A piece of waxed paper, folded at top for strength, is placed over the block and pressed through the nails; it will be used to transfer the complete inked drawing to all the other blocks. Ink the key block with black and print on the waxed paper. Now

key block

Inked waxed paper is pressed down on an uncut block

lift the waxed paper up while the key block is taken out and an uncut block the same size is placed in registered position under the inked waxed paper. Press the paper onto the surface of the block. Remove. Again, place the cut key block into place and ink, print again on the waxed paper, pull out key block and insert another fresh block the same size and lay under the inked waxed paper. Print again. You will need a different block for each color unless, for instance, you print a red over a yellow, to get the extra color, orange, as a bonus.

When you have transferred the total design to the number of blocks of wood you need, you are ready to cut those blocks. Cut away all the space on each block except the part that will hold the particular color for that block.

The key block is the line drawing part of the print.

Blue   Orange   Lavender

Carve away all the areas you want to print in one color.

When printing, do a run of one color on each print, let them dry, and start another color. Paper is placed through the nails and taken off and on again until each color is printed on all the prints.

Try out a few print-runs first to see how you like the color. If you don't, you can always experiment with different tones or different colors before printing up a complete run. The back of a tablespoon is used to rub in the ink.

Note: Try not to allow the nail holes in the printing paper to become larger or the registration may get off. Poor registration is seen in every comic book where the color goes outside of the lines that were meant to contain it. If all this messing around and the prospect of cutting all those other blocks bring you down because more than half the creative work is already done, take a break and don't work in long stretches.

Sometimes when work wasn't going as well as I'd like it to, I'd ask someone around the house to go to the store for me and buy a Fifth Avenue Bar, or whatever kind I was hooked on at the time. But the real thing that happened here was that the idea of somebody doing something exclusively for me, to help me work, was all I needed to get over a creative block or encourage me to continue a stage of work that wasn't all that exciting.

THE ONE-BLOCK METHOD OF WATERCOLOR WOODCUT PRINTING

Most multiple-block woodblock printing is done with oil- or water-base inks. As you've read, the inks are limited in color. In watercolor woodblock, you use one block with watercolor, designer colors, or gouache (the latter two are more opaque than watercolor). This way you have the greatest color choice. I have never used oil paint on the single block, but I can't think of any reason why it couldn't be used. After all, the block can be wiped clean after printing with turpentine. Acrylics would be difficult; they dry fast, and it might be hard to clean the block even with acrylic remover.

I think this watercolor method produces the most sensitive kind of color printing there is. Each print is controlled by the artist's hand—designed, cut, and printed. It does not allow you to print up hundreds quickly, however. After the wood is cut and ready for printing, each print might take you as little as half an hour to as much as three hours (for a very large and/or very complex block) to print, depending on size and how fast you make color decisions.

This method was invented around 1915 in Provincetown, Massachusetts. It seems that quite a few women from France were in Provincetown, all doing woodblocks in the traditional multiblock manner. One woman, Ethel Mars, first developed a shortcut by cutting a line with a penknife within one area of a color block and applying different colors directly to both sections. Nordfeldt, who came to Provincetown at the same time (only from England), picked up on Ethel Mars and developed the one-block method. The prints these people made have the most beautiful color tonality and show the best modern color sense I've seen. The traces of white on the print, caused by the grain in the wood, make a sort of consistency. All the colors have a certain amount of tonality guaranteed them because of the regular amounts of white or off-white coming from the paper through the colors. I started picking up these old prints, and a friend gave us some. I have no idea if enough prints could be dug up to form an exhibit, but I do know both the prints and the method are almost lost. Save it from the grave!

My head has been into this kind of woodblock since I saw some of these single-block prints done by an artist living in Monterey, who had learned the method from one of the few Provincetown people still practicing the technique. She told me I didn't have the patience to do them, and, because most everything she said at the time had the ring of truth, I didn't further my interest in any active way. I was curious, though, as to whether I did or did not have the needed patience, or any patience at all (it was like a teachy fly in my head that bugged me every time I ran into those prints). So for many moons, though this kind of printing is the most obvious and simplest thing to grasp, I had only one eye open to all methods of printmaking. Then a woman on the Cape, who is still doing this kind of color printing, opened my other eye by showing me, in five minutes, how it is done.

DOING IT: A carved woodblock is ready to print. The same piece of paper is going to be brought down on the block each time a different color is brushed on the block.

This is where I used to dash to the freezer for another Heath Bar. Now I try only to drink caffeine-free coffee at this point in the process. It occurs to me that all the names for candy bars must have been chosen by male chauvinists—Mars Bar, Sugar Daddies, O'Henry, Babe Ruth, Three Musketeers, Peter Paul's Mounds, Mr. Goodbar, and M & M is probably for Mister and Master. The rest are neuters, like Old Crows, Twisters (licorice), Hershey Bars, Milky Ways, etc., and there is only one Lady Finger, and it's a kookie cookie. I should start chewing gum.

There are a couple of ways to attach the paper. You'll probably invent ways for yourself after you get into it. If the block you're using is totally carved, with the image filling the entire surface, then an extra strip of wood, 2 inches wide and almost as thick as the block you are using, is nailed

Completely carved block with an extra strip of wood nailed on for attaching your paper.

to the top of the block (almost level with its surface). Nails can be angled in from the underside. The reason I say "almost level" is that you might want to rub the top edge of the block to make an edge impression, and, if you do, it will be easier this way. Place a strip of paper on the top edge of the printing paper for added holding power and thumbtack it to the side of the strip. Press the paper into the right angle as it folds over the top of the board so it will come down flat. A good idea, but optional, is to fold another piece of paper over the edge of the paper on the opposite side of the

thumbtacked edge. A few paperclips will hold it on. It will protect the printing paper from getting messed over by paint on hands while working, etc. Another way to attach the paper is to use a block larger at the top than your finished carving will be (larger at the top because that's where the paper is attached). Paper can be thumbtacked right on the top surface of the block above the woodcut.

COLOR AND BRUSHES: If you are going to use watercolors, try to use those that say "artist's colors," meaning in most cases that they are the best of the two or three lines every company manufactures. The best usually comes in small tubes, and one of these is Winsor & Newton Artist's Quality, which ranges in cost from 65¢ a tube to $1.65. The difference is in the color. Cadmium colors are always best because the pigment is permanent, will not fade, and is more condensed; therefore, you use less of it. You will only find them in greens, reds, and yellows. Look at the color on the chart, pick out the colors you want—like, need, flip you out, and turn you on the most. Select colors that will somehow give you the full range. If you're short of cash, a red, yellow, and blue, those good old primaries you remember from school, can be mixed to give you a full range. Get a medium (true) red, the lightest yellow (the yellow with least orange in it), and the bluest blue (this is ultramarine). What these basic colors can't give you when mixed together to get other colors is the intensity and purity you can get direct from tubes. A white and a black are also necessary to darken, lighten, or gray any color.

Because watercolor dries quickly, one color at a time is applied to the block and printed, using the back of the spoon. There is no rule. If there isn't enough color transferred to the paper, you can do it over—colors can be reprinted and the color can be made darker, generally by adding a touch of black, or lighter, by adding Chinese white. You can even print another color hue entirely over the first one.

This kind of color printing lends itself best to realizing color. Each print can have totally different color. You can experiment with placement of color until all the colors work together, without having to cope further with the problem of changing shapes, their sizes and placement (though, granted, being able to change a shape might help get what you want with color). A fine painter told me she would set up a color structure and put each color in a different size square—some very large and some small. Then she'd use these colors again and again, moving them around in the squares. The effect is individual in each case, and she learned all there was to learn about what those particular colors could do.

Any color, by itself on a white surface, looks good. It has room to expand its identity. Each additional color you add will alter the first color's appearance. The aim is to alter it so you are still satisfied with the first color. It is hard to put down many different colors without the colors destroying each other. Remember this each time you add a color so you won't settle for less. They have to be chosen carefully so they amplify (add another dimension) and sustain one another.

Each watercolor is placed on part of the block directly with a watercolor brush. Red sable brushes will last a lifetime and hold together well. Also, and most important, they continue to have good spring-back. They are the most expensive brushes you can buy, just like a sable coat is the most expensive fur (fifty to a hundred thousand capitalist pig dollars!). When I went to high school, they used to pass out a new red sable brush every year. You were allowed to keep your old one. I am still using those brushes from a pre-Aquarian age. Well, if taken care of, they do last a long time. Other kinds of brushes I've bought have come and gone, and never could be relied on to do what I wanted them to do. Red sables run from $1 to $8 for small to medium sizes. You probably won't need more than a No. 2 and a No. 5—but that will depend on how fine the areas on your woodblock will be—and how large. If you need larger brushes, you can use either oxhair or sabeline, which are less expensive wash brushes. A large No. 24 pure red sable brush costs about as much as the coat, and only Salvador Dali can afford to Dilly-Dali with those . . .

RAISED WHITE LINE OPTION: After a section of the block has been transferred to paper, apply water with your brush directly on the cut-out lines. Bring the paper down on the block and rub the lines with the back of your spoon. This will raise the paper at the line because the paper has been pressed into the line.

WET PAPER BEFORE PRINTING OPTION: Something that might suit your purpose could be using wet printing paper to get softer and blurred edges on your print. These prints sometimes look slightly like watercolor painting. Heavier paper can be used for this one. After the printing paper is wet, press it between newspaper and use as usual.

MUSIC AND COLOR

Everyone recognizes the analogy music has with color: you can think of a flute evoking yellow, a bass evoking blue, or even an oboe evoking dark orange. You can even go so far as to say F-sharp evokes purple. It is also common knowledge that certain color schemes can reflect different moods and emotions just like certain music. Musicians talk about how Impressionist paintings remind them of Debussy. Painters have painted pictures expressing how they feel about jazz, and musicians have written compositions expressing how they feel about paintings (Mussorgsky's "Pictures at an Exhibition," etc., etc.). Besides relating color to music, there has been much talk about rhythm relationships and symbolic psychological relationships between the two forms of expression. The idea that light and sound frequencies stimulate visual and auditory perception was studied long ago.

When he plays his music, Taj Mahal thinks of his sound as a shape. He especially likes the pure forms of Brancusi and Arp because he feels an analogy to the way a note can swell and mold itself into shape and volume. That must be what is meant by pregnant sound, or when your music teacher told you to play a full note.

Going a little farther than the above in the comparison of music to color is not so common... but it is possible to think of a particular color sequence as being just like a particular musical sequence. Being able to do just that is not my purpose, but being able to think of color in some kind of organized way, as musicians do with musical notes, will stimulate a sensibility to the full range.

Using the ordinary colors you see in nature exclusively, like skin color, grass-green, barn-red, is analogous to musicians' using only thunder sounds, bird calls, or the sounds of a truck coming up the road. The fact is, music has been so much ahead of color that it was put into a man-made scheme (88 notes on the keyboard) centuries ago. It is easy to distinguish one of these notes from the others when you hear them. The intervals between notes in Eastern music is so close that, as Tim Hardin says, Chinese children can't sing their own national anthem until they are twenty-five but they can sing "Silent Night" right off. This is the reason Tim thinks the Western system of music is the perfect system. Everyone can sing it. Thinking of color without intervals is thinking of an unharnessed force, just as sound was before musical scales were invented. Imagine what experimenting must have been like for the Pre-Columbian with his three-hole clay whistle—and that's just about how primitive learning color is in the beginning.

There is the Color Harmony Manual with its 900 separate color intervals in chip form adapted from the Ostwald theory, but it has been discontinued by the Container Corporation; however, you can still get Basic Color, by Jacobson, based on the Ostwald theory. Anyone can start thinking of color in terms of the distances between colors and the amount of black and white that can go into each color. For instance, it is obvious that blue is a long way from yellow, and white is a long way from black, but closer measurements of color can be a tool in your mind much as Do-Re-Mi-Fa-Sol-La-Ti-Do is in sound.

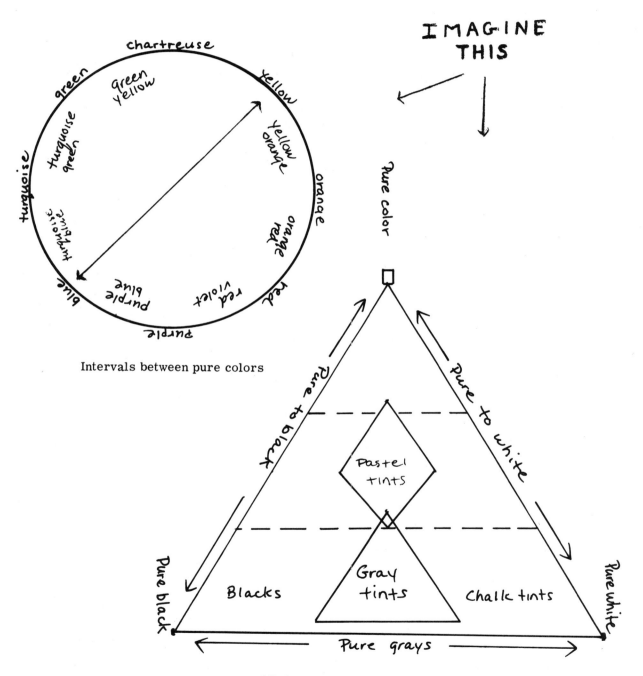

Intervals between pure colors

Mixing a color with white, black, or gray

Single color choices are made from a potential of more colors than there are tones in a music scale. It can be done with less sweat than you'd think. For instance, you can choose color hues out of a certain range of lightness or darkness (tone), which will give your picture a certain all-around tone. You can choose colors that hang around each other, like different hues of blues and blue-greens, which will give the picture a cool feeling. Being aware of color possibilities will make you conscious of when and where you want to limit color.

What is exciting to me is to see a color combined with others so that it appears to be another color than what it really is. A very tuned-in color that does this becomes unique and powerful. These colors have an effect beyond their separate individuality. For example, if only the warmer colors are used in a picture, such as yellow-green, yellow, orange, and orange-red, solid black or black-gray will appear bluish in the same picture (if it doesn't occupy too much space). The same applies to a green mixed with a touch of black (it will appear bluish, as will a red-orange— it will look for all the world like a purple-blue!). Also, a deviation from any group of close colors (such as bright or dark yellow, yellow-green, yellow-orange, orange) will suggest to the imagination a color more brilliant than it actually is. If you use a light pink with the above colors it will appear the dominant color, even if it is a very small area of the picture. You will see when you do it.

Older painters harmonized one local color with another until Rubens' innovation in the seventeenth century. Roger Fry, the good friend of Virginia Woolf, said, "In the golden key of some of Rubens' compositions, a touch of gray made by mixing black and white will count as a definite blue, or the dullest earth-reds will shout like vermilion."

Color can be dissonant in the smoothest, least obvious way, much as in modern classical music or in Coltrane and jazz, when you choose colors that jar, that are close together. It is also interesting to think of using color in places like feedback in music. Feedback can't be notated because there are no notes for it, and a color that is augmented so slightly (slurred into another shade or intensity or into another color entirely) will act much the same as feedback.

Something along this kind of thinking will give your one-block color prints a head start in showing an awareness of color. Since you can actually experiment more with color than with forms (you can't recarve blocks as easily as you can simply print them with different color) you will discover a new excitement in color.

The most interesting kind of inspiration happens when you find some unique quality in your work. It can happen that your whole plan worked out right or that you're surprised at what you did that was accidental. I hope woodblock will be a medium where you will be inspired by your own work.

good
energy,
Jean

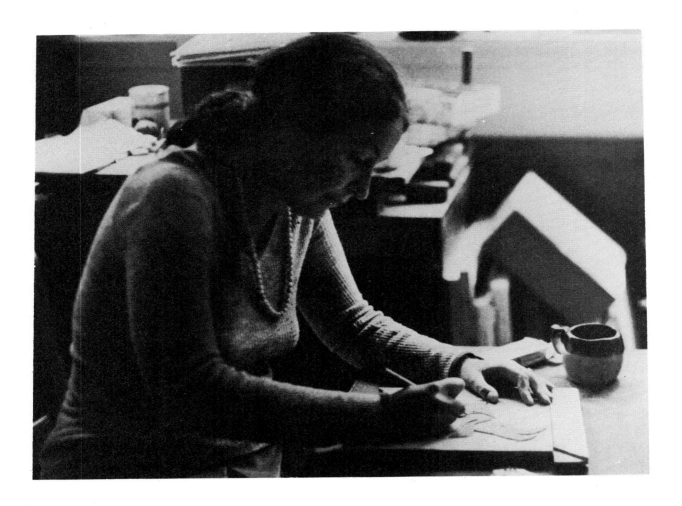

Bronzeworking

Checko Miller

ILLUSTRATIONS AND ASSISTANCE BY SANDEE SHAW

Why bronze? First of all, it is a strong metal, yet easily worked with the aid of an oxygen-acetylene torch. It can be polished to shine and look like gold; it can be left to dull into an earthy hue, or, with the aid of chemicals, appear as copper and very dark. Also, this alloy is relatively easy to obtain and is inexpensive—around $2 a pound. Bronze can last for thousands of years.

With developed skills and proper tools, you can create, from rigid hard metal, fluid shapes with which your imagination tells a story. Designs are created by joining rods of bronze together or combining the fluid, melted form with the rigid rod: concrete realizations of forms from your mind.

What really inspired me to work in bronze was not so much the final product, but watching Sandee, a craftswoman working in bronze. My initial involvement with Sandee was not directly related to her bronze. However, I soon found myself fascinated with her work. The closer I felt to her, the closer I felt to the bronze... the closer I felt to the bronze, the closer I felt to her, and, within this magnetic energy, all were brought closer to one another. When you see the torch being handled right you sense that the assurance and skilled movement are directly related to your own eyes. If you think because you see it you can do it, you're right. You can! Bronzeworking: the art so graceful you feel you are actually seeing what it takes to make it happen. Actually you are feeling it! You are hooked! If the opportunity arises for you, don't pass it up.

1. Gentlemen prefer bronze

I had to try it myself. But after I first wielded the torch, a new insight presented itself: it is not so easy to translate your ideas and feeling into a piece of work. I had always considered metal simply something machines were made of, something merely functional. Now I've come to know it can be a very creative medium to work in. Bronzeworking is not the simplest of crafts, but the rewards from it more than balance out the effort. The concentration put forth creates a new world for you, and it is not one of escape, but one of birth, a real sphere of your own. As your ability increases, the inner satisfaction and confidence increase. Soon you can be making belt buckles, chains, rings, bracelets, hair pieces, pendants, and pins. You don't have to limit your efforts to male-female jewelry either. I know this welder in Laguna, California, who made a bronze chair; another in Provincetown, Massachusetts, made a fantastic toy tricycle about eighteen inches tall. Both people are really involved, but there are all kinds of other projects like soap dishes, animal sculpture, faces, just designs like God's Eyes that aren't hard to do. If you have an inclination to make something different, try it. Do what makes you happy.

ABOUT EQUIPMENT

Getting the equipment means spending some money, but once you have acquired some skill in bronzeworking it's possible to sell your work and then regain the initial investment.

Most of the materials and tools are relatively easy to acquire. Some money is involved, though there are always ways of cutting down on costs. Certain materials are not immediately necessary and some you may already have. The basics cost under $200. A really nice shop costs under $500. You can cut down on the equipment cost by exploring old barns, attics, cellars, the dump, and junk yards; or try purchasing secondhand tools, tables, benches, etc., from friends. Also, keep your eye out for any garage sales and auctions. Try and get to use equipment in industrial arts shops, in schools, in auto-body repair places—or maybe the person next door has an idle torch in the garage. Enough money for rapid acquisition of tools will get you started quicker, but searching for good deals is always an adventure; in fact, the whole bronzeworking trip is an adventure.

A BRONZEWORKER

A bronzeworker can be lost from the rest of the world for hours, with a torch in one hand and uniform bronze rods in the other. The metal melts this way and that way—flux (don't let this new word put you off, I'll elaborate shortly) is sprinkled with a sizzle on the hot metal. Bronze is added, removed, hammered, and cooled according to touch and feel. There is a steady concentration, with hands guiding the tool—be it the torch, pliers, hammer, saw, or polishing equipment. Behind the dark goggles the bronzeworker may appear strange—invisible eyes guiding the hands. How does it all come about? Once you try it the strangeness evaporates through your own self-discovery. You can no longer observe the strangeness, you <u>are</u> the strangeness. If you get off on that, well then get it on.

THE SHOP

Your working area should include certain basic things arranged in a handy way. First, build or obtain a large and <u>flat workbench</u>. It is pref-

A. Hardwood stump with anvil	K. Flux sprinkling jar
B. Bench clamp	L. Flux can
C. Vise	M. Ring mandrel
D. Hotplate	N. Bowl of water
E. Pyrex pot	O. Steel for supporting ring mandrel
F. Bracelet mandrel	P. Steel plate
G. Jeweler's saw	Q. Torch
H. Ring sizers	R. Clip
I. Pliers	S. Drawer or shelf
J. Hammers	

2.

erable to cover the bench with asbestos sheeting, obtainable at a lumber yard, to avoid burning the wooden bench with the torch flame.

Next, get a steel or iron plate large enough to work on; a 9- by 12-inch piece will do. A junk yard or dump will usually supply this item. I use the top plates from an old wood stove, found in a barn. This is one item you shouldn't have to dig into your pocket for.

The lighting where you work is important. It should not cast shadows on the area or cause any glare. A good position for the light source is above and just a little in front of you.

Good ventilation is also important. Make sure that it is adequate. When using a fan in the shop, place it far enough away so as not to affect the torch flame.

You should have a spring clip like those used for brooms attached to your bench so that you can put the lit torch somewhere and leave both hands free. Attach it so that the flame will be aiming in a direction away from you and everything else but air. A burn from a torch is not something you'd soon forget. The clip is also used to hold the torch, freeing both hands for shaping the bronze.

3. The set-up: torch attached to the bench by a clip, bronze rods, and hammers. To get the photo in focus, we had to show the torch pointing more or less toward Sandee. This should never happen in your shop

A piece of <u>peg board</u> is good for keeping tools in order and out of the way when not in use. A lumber yard will be able to supply you with this. You might enjoy making the hooks for the peg board yourself out of bronze. If you ever need a hook with screwable threads, you can easily make one by attaching a hook-shaped piece of bronze to a common screw by joining them with your torch.

A <u>pan of water</u> handy on your bench is good for cooling hot bronze in a matter of seconds, when you need to handle it right away. If you can cool it naturally, though, do, for the above method tends to make bronze brittle.

I should mention that a <u>small vise</u> attached to the bench can also be a valuable addition to your working area. Besides holding materials firmly it can be used to straighten irregularly shaped rings, etc. Place a thick piece of cloth in the vise and the bronze in the middle and then tighten. The cloth keeps the vise from scratching the metal and holds the piece more securely.

MATERIALS AND TOOLS

If you can't find a welding-supply store in the Yellow Pages, information on where to find materials can be obtained through several sources. Inquire first at a plumber's or at a gas station or auto-body repair shop.

The bronze you'll use is brazing bronze, and it comes in rods of varied thickness. Flux-coated rods are better for sculpture, where a lot of heat is used. Uncoated rods work best in jewelry-making. For best selection and economy, go to welding-supply stores.

The <u>flux</u> can be purchased where you buy the bronze and gas. Flux is like powdered glass. It gives the metal an easier and more even flow when you are joining two pieces together. Flux also helps prevent the metal from burning. If the metal spits, blackens, or wrinkles, you are burning it. Sprinkle flux on the area with your fingers or an empty spice jar with small holes. Garlic-salt jars are about right because the holes match the flux particles. Flux is also useful to help clean the piece you are working on. Slightly heat an area, sprinkle flux on, and let it melt into the metal. This process can clean, smooth, and correct burned areas all at once. It is also good when you wish to blend connections more smoothly once a design has been executed.

You have to be quick in removing the flame once the flux melts into the bronze or you will change the shape. When joining or connecting a piece of rod, heat the end of the rod slightly and dip it into a small pile of flux on the asbestos. Flux will not adhere unless the surface is heated first.

The following tools can also all be obtained at a welding-supply store:

The oxygen-acetylene torch used to melt the bronze comes in several sizes and styles.

I suggest one that is light in weight, so it can easily be held steady. Torches are sometimes sold in kits. These include a cutting tip. You won't need this unless you plan on cutting steel or iron bars or plates. If you have ever thought you'd like to change your car into a camper, like I have, you'll want that cutting tip. Also included are torch tips in several sizes. Larger tips give you a hotter flame. The kind of work and rod size you use will determine the tip you'll need. If you're going to do jewelry work, you'll want small tips: 00, 0, and 1. A finer flame allows the beginner more time to develop control. Check what sizes come with the kit. If they are not the right size, ask to exchange them.

The hoses and gauges that come with the kit are essential. Make sure that the hose is long enough. Before you buy the torch set-up, figure out where you want your tanks placed in your shop area. Make sure the hoses will reach.

TIP

OXYGEN-ACETYLENE TORCH

HANDLE

VALVES

HOSES

4.

Before leaving the welding-supply store with your tanks, hoses, and gauges, ask them to show you how to set up the gauges on the tanks. Don't leave until you are sure you understand exactly how they are operated. Don't plan on figuring it out yourself or on asking your friendly neighbor who knows how to fix his lawnmower or truck with baling wire.

You'll need a <u>crescent or adjustable wrench</u> to attach the gauges and hoses to the tanks. From time to time the torch tip will get clogged. So make certain to have <u>tip cleaners</u> about. When cleaning the tip, select a file tip cleaner that fits into the hole where the flame exits. The fit should be snug. Move the cleaner in and out several times and then light the torch to see if you get the proper flame. It should come straight out, not aiming off at an angle or split into several flames.

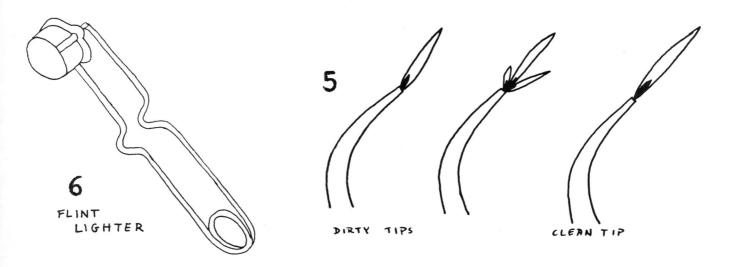

6
FLINT
LIGHTER

5

DIRTY TIPS   CLEAN TIP

To light the torch, use a <u>flint lighter</u> made especially for this purpose. They are also handy for lighting old gas stoves when the pilot light doesn't work. Get an extra supply of flints when you get the lighter. When lighting the torch, hold the lighter within an inch of the tip; rubbing the flint against the steel grater will make sparks to ignite the gas.

The welding-supply store carries the <u>dark protective goggles</u>. You'll need them any time you work on the torch. The bright light from the flame and the hot metal that might spit at you necessitate their use. A pair of <u>clear protective goggles</u> will be handy in other operations, like grinding and polishing. The nose needs protection. Constant exposure to bobbing compound, ammonia, liver of sulphur, and other potential irritants I will tell you about calls for the use of a nose mask. For complete protection you can use a welder's mask, but I find them burdensome, and the shades are too dark.

You'll also need two pairs of <u>pliers</u> with insulated handles.

One pair should be needle-nose and the other flat-nose. Both are good for bending warm metal (cold metal is stiff) and for holding short pieces of rod being melted. Heat gradually moves up the rod to your fingers as you work, so pliers solve the problem of burnt fingers. And they should be small enough to be easily operated with one hand. You can't always find good ones at hardware stores, so also check the craft, hobby, or art stores in the area. Oil the pliers occasionally so that they continue to move easily and to prevent rust. Remember, too, that damage to the pliers will occur if the torch flame comes too close to them. If this happens, a grinding wheel or file can sometimes repair them.

Plier Tips

Flat-nose   Needle-nose

7.

A <u>ball-peen hammer</u> is used to flatten the metal. Both the flat head and rounded end should be smooth to avoid marking the heat-softened metal. A grinding wheel, file, or sandpaper are good to have to keep the hammer in good condition. Avoid hammering on any steel surface directly because this will scar your hammer. A suitable size <u>steel anvil</u>, depending on how large the work is, is the other half of a hammering operation. Always keep any bronze you are flattening between these two steel surfaces. For some purposes, as will be seen later, a hardwood stump or log is better than an anvil. Metal should be warm-to-hot when you hit it. Never hammer molten or cold bronze. Molten will splatter, cold might crack in weak

8. using the ball-peen hammer for cup-making

areas. It may take a while before you can hammer efficiently and accurately. (It's in the wrist.)

There are different ways of hitting the metal. It's not just a matter of striking it. In delicate situations it's better to hit it several times lightly than once hard. It is best to approach metal thinking that you're going to hit it several times rather than to try to get right with just one shot. If you are flattening a small area, you can strike it coming straight down on the piece; when flattening a large area, though, you might try coming in at an angle so that when you strike you can move the metal toward the outside edge.

The round head of the hammer can be used to make curved pieces or cups of metal. Keep hammering the center and it will curve up—heating it, hammering it, heating it, and so on. Interesting effects on flat surfaces are achieved by striking the metal all over lightly, making slight indentations.

Remember, any time you flatten metal you are also making it thinner, and more sensitive to heat. Thin metal reaches a molten state quicker; therefore, you must be more careful whenever you heat flattened metal.

Never hammer bronze until the flux is removed, which you do by heating the metal in a sulfuric acid solution. The acid can be obtained at some automotive-supply places. Mix the solution in a Pyrex container: 10 parts water to 1 part acid. Add the acid slowly to the water—never the reverse, or it will explode. This operation should be done with plenty of ventilation, for the fumes are dangerous to inhale in any quantity. Use a small electric hotplate or electric stove (gas stoves can crack some glass). Or you can put the Pyrex pot in another (ordinary) pot full of water and heat the acid indirectly that way. Slowly heat a solution of acid until boiling in the Pyrex pot and drop your piece in for a few seconds. Remove it from the acid with pliers and drop it into a pan of water that has an adequate amount of baking soda—2 cups of water to 2 heaping tablespoons of soda. This neutralizes the acid. Be very careful handling the undiluted acid, as it burns. If you spill it, pour on a lot of water or milk quickly. Be sure to store it in a labeled container.

A rawhide hammer is useful in reshaping a piece once it is polished. Rawhide will not mark the metal. This inexpensive hammer is good to have, but not essential. Never use it on hot metal.

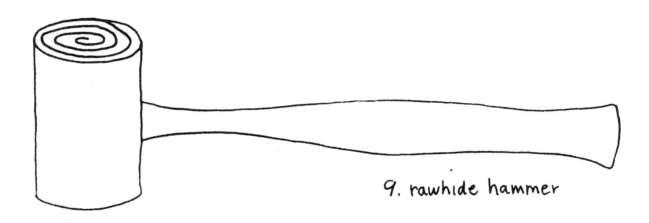

9. rawhide hammer

Files, as previously mentioned, are good tools, too, both for repairing other tools and shaping the bronze. Files are good for smoothing sharp or rough areas, and, in a pinch, they can function in the place of a grinding wheel. When working on a piece with the torch, don't fuss over an area you can fix later on with a small file and grinding wheel. If you don't have a grinding wheel, you must have both large and small files. You'll need both round and flat files, all of finer grades, for if files are too coarse they'll grab the metal. Six-inch hand files are suitable for jewelry-making.

Sometimes you'll use a clamp or vise to hold a piece while filing. Files are designed to work away from you on the forward stroke only. Start at the tip of the file and work toward the handle (see Fig. 18), exerting firm pressure in that direction. In order to make edges of a piece parallel, rub them across the file placed on a work bench (this is especially good for rings).

Grinding wheels are obtainable from most craft suppliers. You might also check with a jeweler, who might just have a good second-hand one for sale. Hand-cranked models are available, but a motor-driven wheel is vastly superior. The latter leaves both hands free, and this makes for much greater control.

Grinding wheels are also good to have around for sharpening kitchen knives or garden tools. Discs of different coarseness come with the wheel. For jewelry, use a finer grindstone. Usually the edge, or primary grinding area, is coarser than the sides. The sides are good for smoothing tools, such as the head of a hammer.

10. Motorized Grinding / Buffing Machine

A <u>buffing wheel</u> attached to the shaft of your grinding wheel makes polishing and smoothing faster and easier. If you are going to purchase a grinding wheel, get one that has a long shaft so that you can connect a buffing wheel. Polishing a piece by hand is more involved—but, I find, better for one's head—than wheel-buffing.

A <u>jeweler's saw</u> is another useful tool, for removing sections of bronze, or for resizing rings when, for example, you want to make a ring band smaller. I find medium grade blades work fine for most cutting purposes. To put a blade in a jeweler's saw, tighten one end of the blade into the compressing thumbscrew farthest from the handle. The teeth of the blade should be facing toward the handle and outward. Press the curved metal arm of the saw against something solid so as to shorten the distance between the two compressing thumbscrews. Tighten the blade into the screw by the handle and relax the tension so that the blade becomes taut in the saw. It will take a little practice to get this operation down. When the blade is at the proper tension, it will make a pinging sound when plucked.

thumbscrew

POSITION FOR
SAWING

thumbscrew

wing screw

Jeweler's Saw

11.

POSITION FOR
PUTTING BLADE IN

You may find it easier to start a cut with a few upward strokes, but the actual sawing is done with downward strokes. When sawing, hold the saw frame in a vertical position. This helps to control the sawing and minimizes blade breakage. Let the blade make its own cut; do not force the blade or exert strong forward pressure. Too much pressure and the blade will break.

There are two ways to remove the blade from a cut after sawing partially through a piece. Either move the saw blade up and down while backing out along the cut, or loosen the wing screw, release the saw blade from one end of the frame, and pull the blade through.

When a shape is to be cut from the center of a piece of bronze, the first step is to make a dent with a center punch or nail. Drill a small hole through the dent with a hand drill or flexible-shaft machine (see below). The dent will prevent the drill from slipping over the surface of the metal. Release the saw blade from the end of the frame, insert it through the hole, and tighten it back into position. Proceed with sawing in the usual manner and, when it is completed, release the saw blade once more and remove the cut-out metal.

A flexible-shaft grinding machine is the best all-around jeweler's tool and is a necessity in your shop if you plan on large production (one good model by Foredom costs about $100). It's similar to a dentist's drill. Many attachments come with this machine, such as: grinding wheels, sanding wheels, wire wheels, rubber wheels, drills, buffing wheels, sanding discs, brushes. These are all good for doing fine work or getting into small areas. The flexible nature of the tool enables you to do much more than can be done with hand files.

12. Flexible-shaft grinding machine with attachments

While using a flexible-shaft, you should be careful not to get the shaft too hot and, whenever it does, to let it cool for a while. It comes with a foot pedal that enables you to vary the speed. The harder you press, the faster it spins. Important: wheels come in both left- and right-hand models. Get the correct one, otherwise the wheel will spin toward you, throwing off particles in your face. Wearing a nose mask will prevent you from breathing in particles and fine dust.

THE TORCH

The flame of the torch consists of two ignited gases mixed together, oxygen and acetylene. By combining them you can produce a flame of 6,000 degrees F.—well above the melting points of all metals.

Getting the proper flame is vital to working in bronze. First you must have the proper pressure settings on your tank gauges. This pressure setting varies with the size tip you use and the style.

		Tank Gauge Settings	
Types of Tip	Tip Size	Oxygen	Acetylene
Style 112	0	15-20	3-5
	1	35-40	5-7
Style 145	00	15-20	3-5
	0	15-20	3-5
	1	30-40	3-5
Style (General) except 112 & 145	00	25-35	2-4
	0	25-35	2-4
	1	30-40	2-4
	2	40-50	2-4

To light the torch, open the valves by the torch just slightly, after you have set your tank gauges correctly. With the valves open, strike the flint lighter in front of tip. It might be difficult at first to get the gas lit. This is usually due to an excess of oxygen or not enough acetylene, so lower the former or increase the latter. An orange, yellow, or white flame signifies an excess of acetylene. This flame is wasteful and will not be hot enough for efficient work. Too much oxygen will sound windy or will extinguish the flame altogether. This flame will burn the metal instead of allowing it to flow. (Oxygen is in the mixture to increase the heat.)

While you are trying to get the flame lit, the gas may pop loudly. Don't get nervous, just readjust your valves. The proper flame is light blue with a slight touch of orange. Never get oil or other flammables near the torch. They might explode.

Once the flame is lit, you will notice that within the larger flame there is a small bright blue flame. The hottest area is at the tip of this flame. Hold the torch so that this point is near the metal. The flame and the bronze create a bright white light. As the metal heats, it turns red to reddish-orange, when it becomes liquid. At this molten point it usually has areas of a silvery color. In order to join two pieces securely, both surfaces to be joined must be in a liquid state. Control at this point, as you will find, is essential. Too much heat will cause the two pieces of bronze to separate on either side of the flame. Too little heat and they will not form a secure joint. The smaller the rod you use, the trickier it gets. Larger rods take longer to heat and require a steady hand. I suggest using the second or third smallest size to start. You can control the amount of heat by adjusting the size of the flame and/or the size of the tip. The smaller the number, the finer the flame. Naturally, before you attempt to do anything specific, experiment and get the feel of the bronze.

I am right-handed, so generally I hold the torch in my right hand and the rod in my left. If you haven't used your left hand much, you'll find that the necessary coordination takes some time to develop. But mostly you must develop patience with yourself, which is one of the benefits of this craft. You are establishing a sense of control, coordination, and rhythm between your hands, eyes, and mind.

Gravity is another force at play here. When bronze is in a liquid state, it flows not only with the heat but with gravity also. You might feel that's obvious, but it's important to be conscious of all you have working for you. Each force in the operation is like a part of a symphony.

If you want to remove an area you can't reach with the grinding wheel, hold the piece with pliers, and heat the area until it approaches a liquid state; then shake the piece so the area will fall out.

The heat and flame are something to be very aware of at all times. The plate you work on, the piece, and whatever the torch comes near enough to will be hot! Be cautious, things may not always appear to be hot. If you're unsure about a piece, use pliers and place it in a pan of water first before touching it. The importance of all this caution will be clearer

13. Cutting a rod with the torch

to you after the first time you forget. For some reason I've found that—with a minor burn—if I immediately place my fingers to my cheek, it helps. I guess it absorbs and distributes the heat, I'm not sure, but it works. If the burn warrants it, use ice and cold water. For bad burns, try squeezing a capsule of vitamin E on the area for fast healing and so there won't be any scar tissue. Also (for sometimes the metal will spit) I suggest you wear clothing that covers you well. You will be using sulfuric acid, and so wearing a full-length apron is a good idea.

You'll find out that once you learn how to use the torch the word will spread and you'll soon be asked to do all kinds of crazy favors, like fixing hooks for a gate, cutting kerosene drums in half—they make calypso drums and great indoor fireplaces—and of course everyone will want something done to his or her car. Your new skill will be much in demand and you will be having fun.

FORMING THE BRONZE

Here are some basic methods for forming bronze. For the lack of a better word, blobs or balls will probably be the first method you will encounter. Always use flux when forming a blob or else you will burn metal. You might try dipping the heated rod into the flux and then rubbing it onto the blob you are forming when you don't want the flux all over. Warm the bronze rod end (using flux), heat the area at the end of the rod until it melts off. If it hasn't formed into a ball, heat it some more while it's on the plate. As mentioned previously, this liquid will gravitate toward itself— thus, the blob. When you want to add a blob or ball to a piece, attach the rod to the piece first. Then using your torch separate the two, leaving the amount of metal desired. Sprinkle flux on the area and then heat. The rod will shorten, forming a blob as it does. Placing several blobs near each other requires some doing so that you don't melt previous work. It is important to aim the flame so that it doesn't affect delicate areas. Using a small fine flame will also help your control.

1. join rod to piece

2. melt off at appropriate length

SPRINKLE FLUX THEN HEAT
ALL SIDES SO BLOB FORMS EVENLY

3.

14.

LEAVE A STEM   OR   NOT

Holding the flame so that it warms the metal rod enables you to bend the rod easily. However, there is a method of stretching bronze to make lines with more texture than the plain cylindrical rod. This is called drawing the bronze out, and requires good coordination between your two hands. Your torch flame moves up the rod, just slightly melting the bronze, while the hand holding the rod directs where you want it to go. You'll find that to make a continuous line without a break takes some practice. Drawing metallic lines can follow you into your dreams at night. You may find it helps to sprinkle flux on the heated rod from time to time as you draw it out. Remember, it's also good for smoothing the bronze, but too much flux will tend to make the bronze blob (sometimes you might want to add blobs to break up definite lines, though).

As you are learning these techniques, it will help if you try and visualize the movement and coordination you are trying to achieve with your hands. Don't let frustrations send you away. Believe in the power of the guide inside you.

There will be times when you will attempt to construct some definite form. At other times you'll want to be loose and casual. In both instances, know that the bronze is partially dictating your next move. And you should be as open to the same flexibility as is the bronze. The outcome may be possibly something that (only) you will recognize the significance of, leaving others to use their imagination. In time you discover yourself connected to the bronze rod; when you change it, you change yourself.

Flattening a rod or a partially worked piece involves warming the metal on the anvil and hitting it with your hammer. (Remember to wash off any unfused flux with acid first.) The method is described earlier in the section on tools under "ball-peen hammer." You can flatten out the design or create raised designs on the top of flat surfaces. To make flat areas, melt off a blob large enough to be flattened to the right size and work it flat on the anvil. This requires some hammering. (To repeat: never hammer metal until the flux is removed or it will mark the bronze.)

Sometimes it is handy to attach a rod temporarily to the piece to be flattened to help hold it steady.

Annealing bronze is another method to form the metal. This is done by heating the rod and then letting it cool slowly. This process leaves the cooled metal less brittle. In this way, maybe with the aid of gloves, you can form the bronze rod with your hands. This is also a good approach when you are hammering the bronze repeatedly.

Bronze can also be brazed to copper, steel, or brass. This is an area where you can strike out on your own, after becoming acquainted with bronze.

DOING JEWELRY

MAKING BEADS: To be able to form beads is useful in jewelry-making. Bronze beads look like miniature doughnuts. To make beads for a necklace or bracelet, it is first necessary to heat the rod enough to enable you to bend it. Place one end of the rod against your steel plate at an angle, say 60 degrees. Apply a balanced amount of pressure and heat so that the end curls up and around into a circle. When it just about overlaps, apply flux where the circle will join, at both ends. Aim the flame back and forth between the beginning of the circle and the point where you will connect, until the joint forms by itself. You might find that at first it is easier to hold the two ends of the circle together with pliers. You may not always get the beads even all the way around, but an irregularly shaped bead has a beauty all its own. In every case, make sure there are no sharp areas that might be uncomfortable next to the skin.

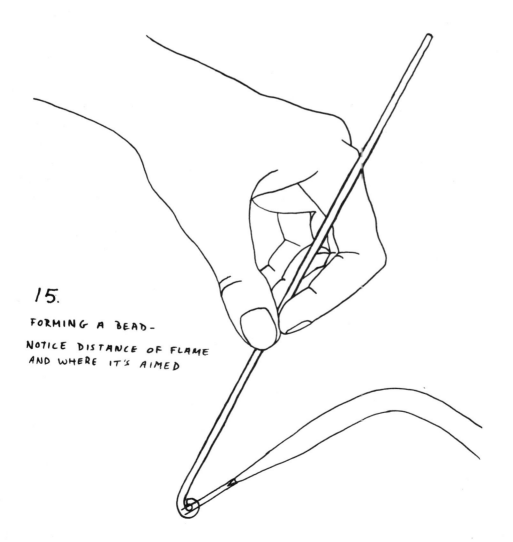

15.

FORMING A BEAD—

NOTICE DISTANCE OF FLAME
AND WHERE IT'S AIMED

To make chains for a necklace or bracelet requires more dexterity. You'll need to pass each link hook through a closed link before joining the ends of the new link. Continue hooking open links into each link you have closed until the desired length is obtained. Keep the flame aiming (only) in the area necessary to join links so you avoid affecting finished areas. You can also insert a solid design in between links.

The ball-and-bead combination is another way of joining movable parts. This arrangement involves a bead or some design that has a hole in it at the end you wish to attach to another piece. To this other piece join a rod that will stick out. Slip the rod through the hole and then melt the rod so that a ball (head) larger than the hole it is inserted through is formed on the end. Sometimes a bead can be hidden underneath a design. You have to be careful not to join the rod-ball to the bead or else the piece won't move freely.

1. JOIN A ROD TO ONE PIECE AND A BEAD TO THE OTHER

2. slip the bead over the rod – see if it swivels easily

3 blob the end of the rod, large enough so that it is larger than the hole of the bead

17.

123

RINGS: One type of ring is a flat band with designs in it that goes all around the finger. Another kind has a design rising above the finger with one or two flattened rods circled underneath.

Study the shape of your finger and how it joins your hand. Each finger is a little different. Study the finger and design the ring to pleasingly fit its form.

In order to make rings, you will need a steel-graduated ring mandrel. This is a tapered cylindrical piece of steel that has the different ring sizes marked on it. You can get one at a craft-supply store. If you want to make a ring to fit someone in particular, you should also get ring sizers. These are bands of steel that are also marked with the different sizes. (A number with a dash after it signifies that it is one half-size larger than the number.) A ring clamp is another handy tool to have. It holds the ring while you're polishing, sawing, or filing. It really isn't essential unless you plan on making a lot of rings.

HOLDING THE CLAMP FIRMLY AGAINST THE BENCH, FILE IN THE DIRECTION THAT IS AWAY FROM YOU. THIS IS THE WAY THE FILE IS DESIGNED

WEDGE

RING CLAMP

RING

FILE

18.

Technique:

Using enough heat to allow the rod to bend, move the flame away from the end as you smoothly and evenly apply pressure to the rod, forming a circle. It is much like forming a bead, only the result is larger. Once you have joined the ends, wash off any flux with acid. Use your pliers and slip the piece onto the mandrel. Get the ring to fit tight on the mandrel by forcing it down with your hammer. This is where a hardwood stump would come in handy, because if you use an anvil the two steel surfaces will damage each other. Set the mandrel on the edge of the stump or log in such a way that the bottom of the band is up against the wood.

POSITION FOR RING MANDREL WHEN FLATTENING

HARDWOOD STUMP

TORCH TIP

BRONZE ROD

19.

RING MANDREL

ASBESTOS SHEET

STEEL PLATE

JUNK PIECE OF STEEL WITH SLOTS

This keeps the band on tight while you flatten it and maintains the ring's round shape.

Hold back on hammering the first side of the band completely flat, for when hammering the other side, some additional flattening will occur in your band. Also, as you flatten the metal, it gets somewhat thinner and the band size increases.

At this point, it is good to have some junk piece of steel that will steadily support the mandrel while keeping the band above the plate. Obtain this by the adventuring-forth method: junk shops, etc. The band of bronze should also fit tight up against this piece of steel to keep it from moving forward.

20. Adding bronze to a ring on a mandrel braced against a piece of junk steel

Begin to add bronze to the band in a design that suits you. You might like to use rods of different widths. Experiment. Variety adds to the beauty. The initial band should be made from one of the smaller sizes. Work first on the larger side of the mandrel, turning the mandrel so that the area you are working on is facing up. As you work, keep in mind that you are creating both a ring and a design.

You will quickly discover that a pot holder, preferably <u>wet</u>, is handy in maneuvering the mandrel. You might have a pan of water large enough to put the mandrel in to cool it occasionally. In the winter it's great to throw the hot mandrel into the snow.

Once you've gotten a fairly satisfactory design on one side, use your hammer to flatten it. You still shouldn't flatten it completely, not until you're finished. This hammering gives you a better idea of how the design will look after the final hammering. Now turn the ring around on the mandrel so that you can complete the design. You may have to tap it off with your hammer. When you've finished the basic design, check all the connections to see if they are good and smooth. To clean and/or blend the design into one flowing piece, add flux to the heated metal and slowly move the heat over the piece, melting the flux in. Remember flux prevents burning the bronze.

If you would like to remove part of the original band to break up any definite line you don't want, do it now. Holding the ring with pliers, heat the area you want removed until it reaches a molten point and shake so that it falls out. You will find that an ability to direct the flame on one area without affecting others is, once again, essential.

Before a final cleaning and polishing, but _after_ removing unfused flux, hammer the ring gently once again to make sure that it is round and smooth. When it's cool, try the ring on. An important aspect is how comfortable the ring feels on the finger. Aside from the smoothing that comes from polishing, you might want to make some changes now.

Another method of making band rings is to work the design out first on a flat surface and, if you like, decorate the outside edge of the design with a piece of rod. This sometimes helps hold the design as you curve it into a ring. Of course, care must be taken if you add a rod for trim, not to affect other parts of the ring.

If you don't have access to a ring sizer, cut a piece of string to the circumference you want. Work out a design and flatten a rod on the anvil to the length of the piece of string. Curve the design as you did the band in the first style. You may want to use your pliers to assist you. Join the two ends together and put it on the mandrel. Make sure that it is securely joined or else it will crack when you flatten and round it out on the mandrel. If you like, finish off by melting the surface into a blending pattern.

To make a ring where the design rises off the finger, you start off by forming a simple narrow band again. The larger the design, the wider the band will have to be. When you're just using a narrow band, it is sometimes a good idea to make the bottom of the ring wider or heavier than the sides in order to balance the top design properly. Once you have the band, add your design using the techniques described in "Forming the Bronze."

Cleaning and polishing your bronze ring is described later; note here though that your files or flexible shaft grinder are used to smooth the finger side of the ring.

For bracelets, you will probably need a bracelet mandrel obtained from craft suppliers. You can make chain or ball-and-bead bracelets that are completely movable, adding whatever slight curve you need with the round end of your ball-peen hammer. However, if you wish to make a bracelet that is one solid piece, you'll need the mandrel. This mandrel is also made of steel (hollowed out) and is tapered; they come oblong or round. It is easiest to construct an open bracelet by starting on a flat surface. Work up your design keeping in mind all the basic procedures. One way is to make a flat design and then a slightly raised design on top of it. Whatever you like. Once this is done, add a piece of temporary rod to one end and curve the bracelet around to join the rod to the other end. Place the bracelet on the mandrel and shape it into the correct curve. The temporary rod you attached can be removed when you get the curve right. The two ends of the bracelet should be either wide or thick so there will not be any uncomfortable edges that will cut into your wrist when you put it on.

To make a hair piece requires no additional equipment. A hair piece can keep the hair back off the face or also hold a section of the hair in place. It has two parts. One is the main part of the design, constructed in such a way that a flat curved bar, the second part, can pass through and out and still be able to turn. The curved bar goes through the design behind the hair and back through the design. Then it's turned around so that it's tight and follows the curve of the head.

21. curved bar and hair piece

128

The opening in the center of the design should be from 2 to 3 inches across and 1 to 2 inches from top to bottom so that the bar will be able to bend and turn. Both the design and the bar have to be slightly curved to fit right.

The bar should be around 5 inches in length, not including any design you might add to it. If you have short hair, find someone with long hair for testing the fit. Keep in mind while working that the bar has to be flat on the design piece in order to lie correctly.

Pendants that hang from around your neck are fairly simple to make. Remember, though, that the hole in the bead the chain goes through should be attached at a right angle to the design so that the whole thing will hang right. Also make sure that the bead is large enough to accommodate what will be passed through it: a leather strip, etc.

Pins are a good way of displaying bronze designs. One very simple method of making them is to curl one end of a suitable length of rod on which you have (maybe) made a design and taper it to a point by pulling the rod as you heat it. Then make a hook on the underside of the rod, at the end, to hold the pin in place. Another method is to make a hinge for the pin by connecting two small beads, standing up side by side, to the back-side. Then insert a rod through them and blob the ends so that the rod won't fall out. In the center of this, connect another longer rod perpendicular to it, and taper it to a point that will go through cloth and fit into a hook on the other side. Make sure to place the pin bar in the top third of the back of the pin.

22. Place bar in rear upper third. Make sure blobs are large enough.

Barrettes can be made in a similar way. Connect two small beads on the back of your design again and run a long rod through them. Bend the two ends of the rod around to the opposite end of the piece and melt off with a blob on the end of each one. Make two small hooks with blobs on the other side, side by side so that they will hold the two transverse rods in place. The barrette itself should have a slight curve to it.

Barrette

23.

the hooks should be connected on the outside and curve toward the inside

    <u>Belt buckles</u> are relatively simple to make also. There are a few important features. The construction of a T shape on one outside edge will be what you connect the belt to. On the other end and underneath, attach a short blobbed rod that will go through the holes in the belt to fasten it tight around the waist. Take note not to have any sharp protruding edges around the outside. The wearer bends over now and then and that buckle could jab.

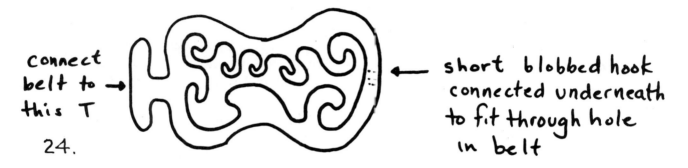

connect belt to → this T

24.

short blobbed hook connected underneath to fit through hole in belt

    <u>Necklaces</u> can be made using any or several chain styles. Chains move and follow the lines of the neck. On the same principle, solid designs can be connected with links. The ball-and-bead combination also is a good way to join movable parts.

    Stringing beads on the thinnest bronze wire or good strong cord can also be attractive. Wooden beads are best made out of hard wood. You can use your grinding wheel to help shape them. You might consider making some ceramic beads with a low-fire clay that can be done in the oven, or you may come across some attractive ready-made beads that you can use in a bronze necklace.

    It will take some doing to get a nicely balanced necklace that lies evenly. The more complicated and intricate the design, the more difficult it is, but that didn't crimp Michelangelo.

25. a simple clasp for a necklace

connect to string or link

Clasps at the back of the neck should be easy for the wearer to connect and comfortable.

FINISHING AND POLISHING

To finish a completed piece, it's good to treat it with a sulfuric acid solution (see the description of this process earlier in the chapter). This treatment gives the bronze a coppery color as it cleans. Dry the piece and polish.

To polish bronze, you will need bobbing compound found at craft stores, but if you use emery cloth you won't need the compound. Rub the compound on your buffing wheel by holding it next to the spinning wheel for a second or two. Keep adding the compound as you need it, but don't put a whole lot at once on the wheel. The buffing process not only polishes and smooths the surface, but it also can be used to change the shape slightly if desired. For more major changes, use the grinding wheel or file. The grinding wheel can add to the form by making indentations into thick areas.

If you have a piece that isn't flat and you would like to give it more dimension or more color contrast, use liver of sulfur. This can be purchased at a craft-tool store. The liver of sulfur reacts with the coppery coloration that the acid makes. To use liver of sulfur, first treat the piece in sulfuric acid. After cleaning the piece in sulfuric acid, put the bronze into the water with the baking-soda solution, then put a small piece of liver of sulfur into warm (not boiling) water. (This should be done in an enamel pan.) Continue to reuse the same liver of sulfur solution until it gets cloudy; at this point the solution has lost its effectiveness. The smell of the liver of sulfur is hardly pleasant, but it quickly disperses. Leave the piece in the solution until the bronze is as dark as you want it. Then rinse with water. Polish the areas you want shiny and leave the rest alone. A solution of diluted household ammonia and soap will clean off any bobbing compound residue on the bronze and your hands. Unlike gold, bronze rapidly oxidizes to a dull finish. This gives it a more earthy and ancient appearance. When you're choosing your design, make sure it will still be attractive when dull. Sometimes not making the bronze completely smooth will leave texture that goes well with a dull finish. To return the shine, use silver polish or even rub the piece on a rug.

Sandee likes to think her bronze work will be discovered a thousand years from now because bronze lasts a long time, but it is enough to fulfill the personal need to create at the moment...I know you will have the same satisfaction working with it as I do.

Bronze, metal, metal of the Earth,
     ancient, ancient in the hands of Man—
    Valued as tool, weapon, wealth, and decoration.
   Stronger than praised gold and silver
    and oxidizing in varied colors,
  Bronze, ancient metal of the Earth
     remains a fascination in my eyes
       for its beauty of strength, color, and form.
Flame, fire heat, burning gas of the Earth
    timeless is the mystification it creates—
  Valued as tool and weapon, as life and death.
    Flame is the music that makes Bronze dance,
     though the melody is formed from the properties
    of each.

In the end Bronze remains Bronze, Flame remains Flame.
The Craftsman uses the power of love heat
   to soften the rigid strength,
 as they, too, use the Craftsman.
   There is a balance of power, a balance of beauty.
Each direct and bend with the nature of each.
For the Craftsman seeing the metal soften into fluid forms,
   it is as if some rigid tension was soothed
     in his own mind,
    as if disjointed thoughts blend together
    in a conception.

There is a romance formed between the
  Bronze   Flame   Craftsman

Tipi-Making

Steve Raleigh and Paul Alexander

"Everything the power of the world does is done in a circle. The sky is round, and I have heard that the earth is round like a ball, and so are all the stars. The wind, in its greatest power, whirls. Birds make their nests in circles, for theirs is the same religion as ours. The sun comes forth and goes down again in a circle. The moon does the same, and both are round. Even the seasons form a great circle in their changing, and always come back again to where they were. The life of a man is a circle from childhood to childhood, and so it is in everything where power moves. Our tipis were round like the nests of birds, and these were always set in a circle, the nation's hoop, a nest of many nests, where the great spirit meant for us to hatch our children. But the Wasichus have put us in these square boxes. Our power is gone and we are dying, for the power is not in us any more." — Black Elk

We got into tipi-making not out of any strong (at the time) interest in Indian lore, but because we'd both had it with camping in tents. We'd been camping together for a long time, and one day we started looking for an alternative. The tipi was an answer.

At first it looked a little difficult, but after we got into it (with the exception of a few minor hitches along the way) it turned out to be pretty easy. The Laubins' book on tipis is the one most people consider the best. When it comes to the history, symbolism, etc., of the tipi as home for various Indian tribes, that book is the best we know of. As for how to make a tipi,

133

we want to offer here detailed step-by-step directions.

So as you won't be put off by what only <u>looks</u> complicated, we'll give you a sort of brief description of a tipi so that you can visualize what you'll be doing before you start yours.

A tipi is basically a cover of material wrapped around a bunch of poles positioned in a tilted frame of three more poles. The cover is made of strips of canvas (or skin, in the old days) sewn together and then cut to form a semicircle. The smoke- and door-holes are cut out of the canvas beforehand. Then the radius point (center of the straight edge) of the semicircle is fastened to the top of a pole, which is then dropped into place on the tilted cone of poles. The canvas is then pulled around the poles until the ends meet, and then laced together.

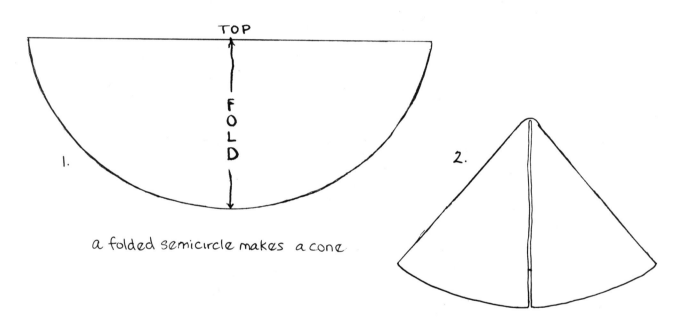

a folded semicircle makes a cone.

When the hole at the top is open, you can build a heating and cooking fire inside the tipi. If the tipi is constructed right, it will be watertight when the hole is closed. We guess we did ours right because, during the first stormy night we spent in our tipi, only a little water got in, and now, over a year later, we're still dry inside when outside it's pouring buckets and the lightning is flashing all around. (We've come to really love the sound rain makes as it hits the tipi!)

That smoke-hole should be just above the center of the circle where the fire is. Somebody once said that living in a tipi is like living in a giant chimney, but this is not really true if you build good fires, and have a good lining around the bottom part of the tipi. Linings also help to keep bugs out. A few of the friends who stayed overnight in our tipi have complained of a spider or two, but they don't know how lucky they were not to have been there while the ants were still around. For the first couple of weeks, we were plagued by ants, but then they just packed up and went away as the earth inside the tipi got drier because of our fires. At least this is probably why they left. But maybe they just didn't like our company.

The lining is like a second cover, but it runs only 6 or so feet up from the bottom of the tipi. It is attached to the inside of the poles with ropes and, in addition to its other functions, it serves as good insulation. We've never stayed in our tipi in the middle of winter (although we will this year), but we know a family of five nearby who've lived in theirs year-round for three years. They have all the conveniences, including a plywood floor, and they say they're warm as toast even in the roughest part of the winter. One of the reasons for this is the lining. People who haven't been around tipis very long think the cover is a complete tipi. It isn't.

The tipi is still used by Indians on reservations, but now mostly for religious ceremonies. Tipis are used by a lot of young people who want to go back to the land. And it's not really roughing it, because with a few books, perhaps a chessboard (we play chess, sometimes all day), and sufficient food, say some brown rice, potatoes, canned and fresh fruit, powdered milk, pancake mix, instant soup, etc., you really soon forget the outside world. We've stayed in our tipi for over a week without having to go out for more provisions. We also had a harmonica, a guitar, and a jew's harp (which no one could ever figure out how to play).

Besides being one of the most beautiful shelters, the tipi also has many advantages over the modern, commercially made tent. The average tipi has more room than the average tent. It is probably the cheapest shelter you can live in permanently, and the biggest advantage is the indoor fire for heat, light, cooking, and beauty.

You should pitch your tipi in a place somewhere near your house and spend weekends, holidays, or whatever out there—or maybe use it as a tent for parties, but we disapprove of this because it is not what a tipi is meant for.

Your campsite should be in a field, near a source of clean water (remember to boil any drinking or cooking water you're not sure of 10 to 15 minutes). The reason for being in a field is so that you get lots of sun; the tipi won't mildew, and sun is great anyway. Falling branches from close trees won't puncture your tipi, and there will be less bugs. Also, if you are under a tree it will keep on dripping on the tipi after a rain (or heavy dew) which causes a very loud and annoying noise.

Tipis can be made in many sizes, starting from about 12 feet in diameter all the way up to 25 feet or larger. We've seen some 30-foot tipis. A 12-foot tipi is not large enough for both fire and people and should be used as a play tent for children, and a tipi much larger than 22 feet is hard to heat and hard to put up, hard to find poles for and hard to move. We feel that an 18-footer is an ideal size, that's why we'll show plans for an 18-foot tipi, although if you want to live permanently in a tipi with a family, you should try for a larger one.

MATERIAL, SIZES, AND AMOUNTS FOR AN EIGHTEEN-FOOT TIPI

CANVAS: We paid for our 18-foot tipi by doing odd jobs—gardening, babysitting, etc., with no financial help from our parents. We split the cost right down the middle as well as the work. Altogether it cost us about $75 for canvas (this was first-rate canvas) and another $25 for odds and ends.

The cover and door-flap will take 39 1/3 yards of 72-inch duck. The canvas can be purchased at various weights, the lightest being about 8-ounce duck, and the heaviest up to 16-ounce. The lightest is naturally the cheapest, and if you plan to move your tipi a lot, use a 8-to-10-ounce, lightweight canvas. If your tipi is going to be set up in a place where there are a lot of storms and as a semipermanent placement, then use a heavy-weight canvas, 12-to-14-ounce. We recommend 10- and 12-ounce, which is the weight usually used, as it works for almost any weather and is not that heavy.

Be sure and get canvas that is already waterproofed. Although it costs a bit more, it is really more effective against wetness and lasts longer. Also you don't have to allow for shrinkage, as you will if you waterproof your own. Should you want to do your own waterproofing, you can buy about 6 gallons, 3 for cover and 3 for lining, of waterproofing at camping-supply stores or hardware stores. Follow directions on the can. Shop around until you find the best canvas for the least amount of money. 72-inch wide will not entail the work and labor that 36-inch material demands, and is more effective. (This is the size our instructions are geared to.)

The lining takes about 17 yards of 72-inch duck. It can be made of lighter-weight canvas and also should be waterproofed (by the manufacturers or by you).

THREAD: The supplier of the canvas should also have thread. Any strong rot-resistant thread will do. I bought mine wholesale in $10 spools. You will need a good 5,000 yards.

TIE-TAPES: These can be made by folding a 3-inch-wide strip of canvas over twice and sewing it down. You can also purchase tapes by the roll from the dealer you buy canvas from. You will need 10 to 15 feet of tie-tape. They will be attached to the top and bottom of the smoke-flaps and tied together, as described later.

PEGS AND PINS: We started collecting pegs while we were sewing the cover and lining. You will need 20 to 25 wooden pegs 18 inches long and 1 inch thick for pegging the cover to the ground. Any hardwood you can find will be good enough. If you know trees, you can look for cedar, maple, ash, oak, or chokecherry.

The pegs are sharpened to a point at one end, and you should leave about 6 inches of bark at the other to catch the rope you will be tying to it. Another way to catch the rope is to carve a ring around the top of the peg.

3. pegs

You need 10 lacing pins (used in buttoning up the cover around the poles). These sticks should be pointed, too, and about 12 inches long and 3/8-inch thick. Lumber yards have dowels you can buy and cut to size, but of course that is very un-Indian.

Get together about thirty 2-to-5-inch sticks, 1/4- to 1/2-inch thick. These will be used after your lining is up, and inserted between the rope that ties the lining to the poles and the poles themselves, so that water running down the poles will not get sidetracked and run down the rope.

ROPE: Hardware stores should have manila rope. You need about 45 feet of 1/2-inch manila rope to tie the poles together at the top. To tie the pegs to the bottom of the cover, you will need about 100 feet of 1/4-inch nylon cord. And lastly, at least 200 feet of 1/2-inch cotton rope for tying the lining onto the poles, for the smoke-flaps and a few odds and ends. Don't worry about buying too much, it's impossible. You can always find use for rope later.

MAKING THE COVER

We first tried sewing on one of our mothers' very small portable Singer machine. But it didn't work; the needles kept breaking. We finally gained access to a Sears heavy-duty machine. This worked for us. Probably any good, heavy floor-model number would work for you, though. Some people run long extension cords to their machine so they can work outside. We sewed ours in the winter so we missed this.

A semicircle when folded in half makes a cone. A tipi looks like a tilted ice cream cone upside down (see Fig. 2). The way to make the half-circle is to sew strips together and then, when they are laid out on the ground, cut a half-circle shape out of the big piece as we will explain later.

direction of seams—
side view

4.

front view

First cut 3 strips from the 72-inch canvas. Strip One is 38 feet, 6 inches long. Strip Two is 36 feet, 7 inches long, and strip Three is 30 feet, 10 inches long. It's a good idea to cut them all a few inches longer than you

5.

strip #1	38' 6"	72"
strip #2	36' 7"	72"
strip #3	30' 10"	72"

actually need, just to be safe. Next fold each strip exactly in half and, with a marking pen or heavy pencil, mark the center where it folds, both on the top and bottom of the fold and on both sides of the canvas where it folds.

6.

This makes 4 marks altogether. Roll up Strips Two and Three with a string around them and attach a tag telling which one is Two and which one is Three. Put these away for later on.

7.

STRIP ONE IS THE HEAVY TRIP

Strip One is the strip that you are going to be doing most of the sewing and cutting on. It is the strip that will have both the smoke-flaps and the door in it.

Cut a piece 11 by 2 feet out of each end of Strip One and sew them together so that the piece is then 21 feet, 10 inches long (see Fig. 8). This will be Strip Four to complete the semicircle shape. Roll Strip Four up and label.

measure and cut corners
of strip #1

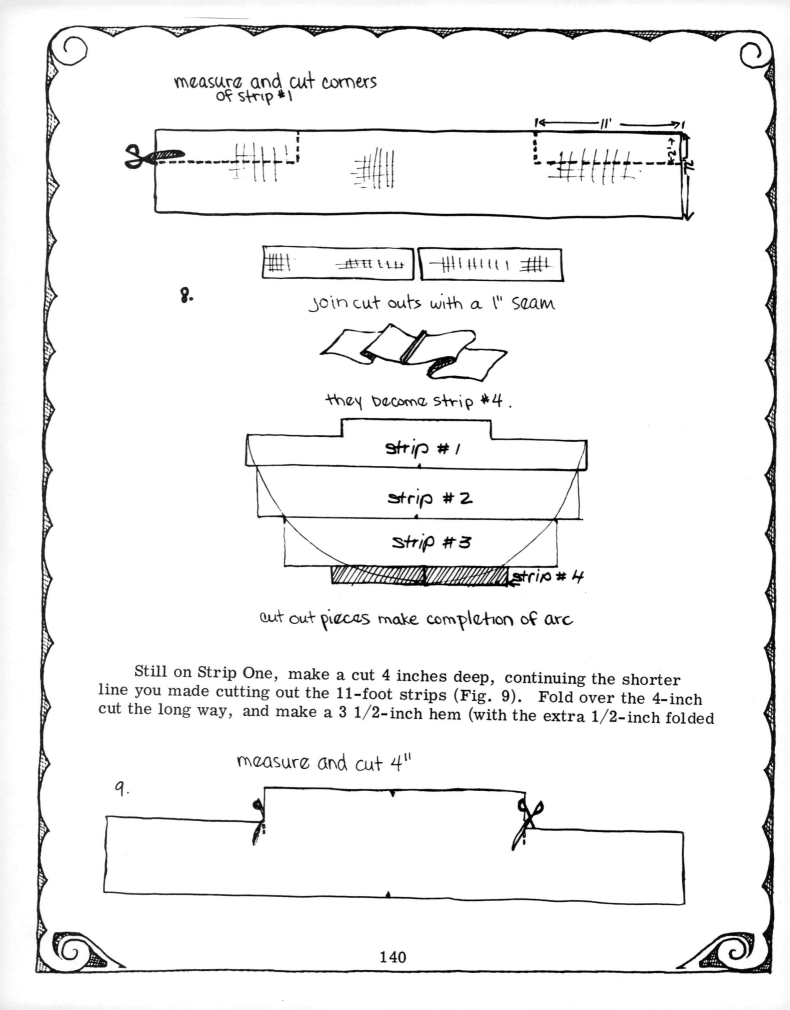

8.

join cut outs with a 1" seam

they become strip #4.

strip #1

strip #2

strip #3

strip #4

cut out pieces make completion of arc

Still on Strip One, make a cut 4 inches deep, continuing the shorter line you made cutting out the 11-foot strips (Fig. 9). Fold over the 4-inch cut the long way, and make a 3 1/2-inch hem (with the extra 1/2-inch folded

measure and cut 4"

9.

under again at the cut edge). With the machine sew the hem down two or three times in parallel lines (double stitching) 1/4-inch away from each other to secure it well (Fig. 10). These 3 1/2-inch folded sections will be where you will make buttonholes in both sides; they will later be attached by lacing pins to hold the cover together.

turn under ½ inch, hem 3½ inches.

10.

After you have sewn the lacing-pin reinforcement down, cut out the two halves of the door. Starting 1 foot from each end of Strip One, on the side where the 3 1/2-inch hems are folded over, cut a semicircle 46 inches long and 10 inches deep at both ends. Sew over a 1/2-inch hem on the same side as you sewed over the 3 1/2-inch hem all around this door-opening area (Fig. 11). The pieces you have cut out can be used later to back the top of the cover for reinforcing.

11.

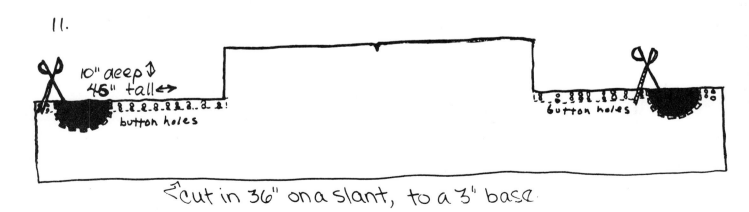

10" deep
45" tall
button holes   button holes

cut in 36" on a slant, to a 3" base.

141

The large center piece in Strip One is going to be the smoke-flaps. Starting at the middle of that piece, cut two lines straight but on a slant, ending 1 1/2 inches to either side of the center, 36 inches from the top (Fig. 12). This will form a narrow triangle when you cut it out, but make sure you leave a 3-inch-wide tab of canvas at the base of the triangle. This tab is what supports practically the whole tipi, and this area should be backed with three or four layers of canvas reinforcement.

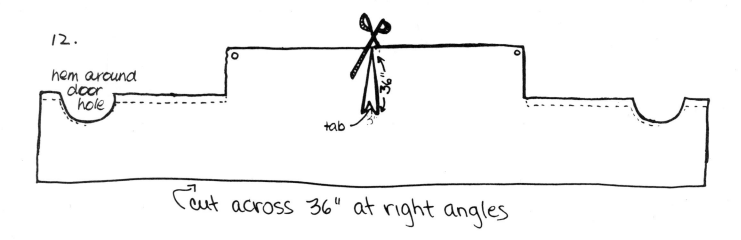

cut across 36" at right angles

At the base of the tab, and to either side of it, cut a line at a right angle to the center line, 36 inches long (Fig. 13). When these cuts are opened up, they form a triangle, on either side. What happens now is that separate pieces of material in a triangle shape (called gores) are fitted into these two triangles and sewn in place with a 1-inch seam again on the wrong side (seam and hem side). Cut the gores 40" x 40" x 9"; this allows for the 1-inch seam, and, when sewn in place, the areas will measure 36" x 36" x 7". Now hem 1/2-inch on all three sides of the smoke-flaps. (All sewing should be in double or triple lines of stitches except for the smaller 1/2-inch hems.)

The tab in between the smoke-flaps is the tie-flap area, and, to repeat, it needs reinforcing. Reinforcement pieces look better if kept on the inside of the tipi because the poles at the top will cover the pieces from the inside. (Remember which is the outside and inside of your cover.) Place two pieces on the inside of the tipi reinforcing the tab area. Sew all over the place with your machine. Some people like to do this by hand.

Attach two 3-foot tie-tapes to the center where the tab is (Fig. 14). Slap another piece of canvas on top of the tapes and sew firmly (Fig. 15). These tie-tapes will tie the cover to your lifting pole (the pole that lifts the whole cover up and onto the rest of the poles). Two more tie-tapes, 1-foot long, are to be sewn at the base of the smoke-flaps in the inside corner (Figs. 14, 15). The tie-tape on the right side of the smoke-flap is placed on the hem side and the tie-tape for the left side is placed on the outside (or right side). When lapped over, they will tie best in this position. These tie-tapes will act as the top lacing pin. Reinforce these too, but not as much as the tie-flaps at the top of the tipi.

tie tapes

14.

outside

15.

reinforcement

Next are the smoke-pole pockets. They must be on the outside. Cut four pieces, as shown in Figure 16. Each pocket will be made double-thick by using two pieces of material together. Hem under the 2-inch edge 1/2-inch and then fold and sew three times so this pocket will hold well (Fig. 17).

pole pockets for smoke flaps

16. 2" 5" 7"

17. fold and sew (double stitching)

Before you attach the pockets to the upper corner of the smoke-flaps, reinforce the smoke-flaps from the outside (poles will hide this later), slapping on a triangle of extra canvas. Then attach the back of the pockets to the corners using many rows of stitching (Fig. 18).

18.

sew pockets so they're on the outside of flaps

Now you are ready to do the last part of this complicated fooling around with the first strip, sewing on the buttonholes! You will need to make altogether 59 holes for the entire tipi so get comfortable: 13 in the lining, 44 to lace together the cover, and 1 on the bottom tip of each smoke-flap (2 in all).

The cover should have 2 rows of 9 buttonholes on each side of the 3 1/2-inch hem area (36 in all), starting near the tie-tape at the base of the smoke-flaps, to the top of the door opening. Add 2 rows of 2 buttonholes (4 in all) on both sides (8 in all) under the door. All should be really round and about 1/2-inch in diameter. Try and space them out evenly. The outside holes should be about 3/4-inch in from the edge. The rows on the left flap should be 2 inches apart, and the rows on the right flap 1 1/2 inches apart. When the left side laps over the right, this variance in distance will make the insertion of the pins easier. The top holes under the door will be for a lacing pin and the bottom holes are there to attach to the ground pegs with rope.

Sewing the holes is difficult because you have to really pull the thread hard. Linen twine (thread) used for sewing braided rugs together is good and strong. You have to go out of your way to get this; large needlecraft-supply houses, boating-supply houses, and sometimes people who deal in leather have heavy threads that will be great for the buttonholes. Actually any tough cotton thread will do. Coat the thread with beeswax, purchased at hardware or sewing stores, thread it on a strong needle with a thin head, and fold double. Twist and coat it again with beeswax. You now have the strongest and most effective thread going for you. There are several ways to make a buttonhole, and we have illustrated the easiest (see Fig. 19). The buttonhole will become almost like a wooden ring. Hammer it to flatten it out on a piece of wood.

lacing up the front

inside layer holes are closer together

detail of buttonhole stitch

19.

There are two more buttonholes to make on the cover: one on each smoke-flap—bottom outside tip (see below). Strings will be tied there to pull the flaps out.

20.

ON TO STRIPS TWO, THREE, AND FOUR

Now you are ready to really move. Get out the second, third, and fourth strips. Here's where that center mark comes in handy. Line the strips up so that the center marks join (see Fig. 8). Start with Strip Four, which shows the center with its seam. Pin Strip Three on top of Strip Four so that center marks meet and so Three overlaps Four about 3/4-inch. Sew them together using two rows of stitches 1/4-inch-apart. After that is sewn down, you can join the center marks of Strip Two and Strip Three, making sure that Two overlaps Three, and sew down. Next is the final piece to sew on: Strip One should be placed overlapping Strip Two with the centers joined up. The reason for the overlapping is so water will run off well and will not get caught up in the seams. It is like shingles on the roof (see Fig. 4).

CUTTING OUT A HALF-CIRCLE FROM THE SEWN STRIPS

Find a flat dirt or grass surface to pin down the pieces you have just sewn together. We used a dirt surface, and the canvas ended up with a lot of footprints all over it, as well as some from the dog and cat. Grass is best if you **have** it around. Stretch it out tight. Drive a stake in the lower corner of both sides of each strip (Strip Four is the bottom strip). Don't

worry about tearing it because this is the waste part that gets cut away anyway. Drive a stake in the ground 25 inches above the tie-tapes. Attach a
19-foot, 2-inch rope. Swing the rope in a semicircle across your material
and mark the end of the rope swing with a piece of colored chalk or a crayon. Cut out on this line and do not hem. You don't have to worry about the
material unraveling along this line because the material is cut across the
bias. The cover is finished, except for minor details you can attend to
while pitching the tipi.

21. marking the lower edge

LINING

Some people consider a lining unnecessary. Wrong. It keeps out most
of the bugs, adds an unbelievable amount of beauty, keeps you much drier,
keeps you warm in winter and cool in summer, and, because it acts with
the cover to create a draft, it helps ventilate the fire, and aids in clearing
smoke out of the tipi. We would not consider living in or making a tipi without a liner.

The lining is hung on a rope stretched around the poles and measures
a little under 6 feet tall. We drew some plans for a lining that is the one
we use (Fig. 22). It is not perfect. If you are striving for perfection, we
refer you to the Laubins' plan for your liner. Their lining is made so
every seam meets at a pole and fits perfectly. Ours does not fit so perfectly and the seams don't correspond with the poles, but it is a lot simpler
to make. We are satisfied with it. The directions we give apply only to our
plan. If you use another plan, follow their directions for an 18-foot tipi.

If you are using 36-inch material for that lining, cut the entire length in half and sew the strips horizontally together to produce a 72-inch width (it will be a little under 72 inches because of the seam). If you are using 72-inch material, you're set. Lay out the strip and cut 10 panels, 5 feet, 7 inches on the bottom, 3 feet, 8 inches on the top as the diagram shows.

lining pattern

22 A.

3'8"

72"

5'7"

If you use 36-inch canvas, you are going to have to make sure that, when you sew the panels together, the center seam overlaps in the same direction on all the panels in that section. If you use 72-inch canvas, obviously it doesn't matter since there is no center seam.

Most linings are made in three sections, which makes putting it up easier. In each section you sew together subdivisions called "panels." On our lining, two sections (#1 and #3) have three panels, and the back section (#2) has four panels. (The Laubins' has 15 panels in all, which gives you an idea of how complex theirs is.) There are buttonholes across the top, which are there so you can attach the lining to a rope that is tied around each pole and strung from pole to pole. The bottom of the lining of our tipi can be secured by pulling it outside of the tipi and placing heavy rocks on it; or you can sew tie-tapes to the bottom and tie those to the poles, but this usually will not work because you cannot be sure if the poles will line up with the tapes.

22 B.

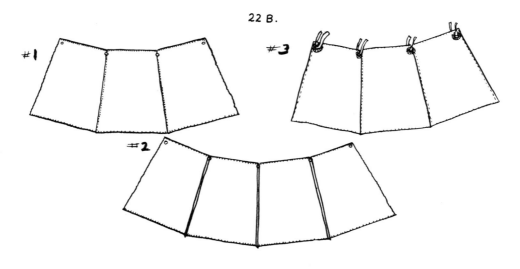

#1

#3

#2

Sew the lining panels with the same thread as the cover. The sections are not to be sewn together. By leaving them open, it is easier to pitch the tipi.

After you sew the panels together, sew buttonholes at the top of each end of a section and one at each seam (all about 1 inch from the top). You will end up with 13 buttonholes. Cut thirteen 6-inch lengths of thin rope or soft leather (leather looks far better than rope). This is to tie the lining to the lining rope when pitching the tipi.

We previously said that the cover looks better unpainted. That is not true of the lining. Almost any tipi expert and all Indians will agree that it is <u>necessary</u> to paint the inside of a lining. But imagine the inside of the tipi at night, fire flickering, black sky with a few bright silver pinholes through the smoke opening, the poles against the light brown, smoke-colored canvas, and, lastly, beautiful Indian designs around the lining. The Laubins' book and almost every Indian craft book has Indian lining designs. Spread the three sections out on a flat surface (if you're outside, place rocks on it so the wind will not blow it around). Draw lightly (with charcoal or pencil) the outline of your pattern, and then paint. Leave the lining exactly where it is until the paint is completely dry.

If you want, you can sew 5 or 6 buttonholes up the sides of section #2 and up one side of sections #1 and #3 so that you can close the gaps up after the tipi is pitched. Sections #1 and #3 are not connected on the side that is near the door.

In the winter, we suggest the use of an <u>ozan</u> to trap the heat at the base of the tipi. An ozan is a semicircular sheet made of canvas. It is attached to the poles and/or lining in such a way that it acts as a roof for the rear half of the tipi.

THE DOOR-FLAP

The door-flap can be made a number of ways, and the only advantage of one over the other is the way it looks to you. Doorflaps can be cut in many shapes as long as they cover the door hole. Cut a shape about 54 inches long and 26 inches wide (where it covers the door area), fanning out to 40 inches wide at the bottom, and narrowing into a triangle shape near the top (see Fig. 23). It should be hemmed 1/2-inch all the way around. The bottom is folded over a dowel or stick and sewn down on the inside, or you can attach the stick to the outside. This will help keep the flap from curling. Nylon rope or any scraps of leather you have lying around can be used to tie to each end of the stick; these can be fastened to stakes in the ground on both sides of the door when you want to tie the door-flap down. You can also handle it as in the photo. Another stick further up can be tied on to the canvas with a strip of leather. Sewing two buttonholes 2 inches apart in the triangle at the top of the door flap will add a third layer of buttonholes to the two sets of buttonholes just above the door hole in the cover. These are joined up by a lacing pin. If you make these holes last, you can line them up and make sure the door comes to the base of the tipi. When the bottom stick is not tied down, the lacing pin allows the door to swing to the side so you can enter. And of course you can take the door all the way off if you like.

inside view of doorflap

buttonholes 2" apart

23.

24. One way to make the door

A STORM DOOR

A good thing to have around is a storm door made from a piece of 4-x-6-foot canvas. When it rains, tie the storm door to the poles on the inside of the tipi, and pull the edges outside at the bottom and tie to pegs. It sheds the water very well.

Whether you paint the cover or the lining, the paint should be waterproof after it is on. The only paints that will be waterproof and durable are oils and acrylics. We suggest acrylics because they will not tend to rot the canvas as oil paint will. The best acrylics can be bought in art-supply shops in tubes or jars by the color. Different colors are different prices so it would be difficult to lay any costs down here for you. Also, we would have to know how much of the surface you wanted to cover. Acrylics are water-based, but after they dry they are permanently proof against weather and water—and have a tough surface. The Laubins' book recommends using casein colors, but casein available on the market is water-based and is not waterproof. If you use it you will have to spray it with a clear plastic.

POLES

Our cover was made in the winter. In the spring we had to start getting our poles together. Getting the poles for your tipi will probably be the most difficult part. One of us still had his leg in a cast when spring came, so the other was alone in getting the poles. It was the hardest part, because from where he lived mountains had to be climbed and each pole dragged back. The poles had to be zigzagged all the way to get them through the heavy forest, and an axe used. It took at least fifteen trips up and back to do it.

The poles should be as straight and as free of knots as possible. When it rains, whatever water gets in through the top will run down the sides of the pole and drain off and away from the tipi. If there are bumps or knots, the water will drip from these and down to the tipi floor.

The larger the tipi, the more poles you need. The tipi we are giving you plans for is a Sioux tipi. It needs 15 poles for the structure, 2 poles for the smoke-flaps. Its diameter is the same as its height: a Sioux tipi 18 feet in diameter is also 18 feet high. The poles should stick up over the top of the finished tipi about 5 or 6 feet. This means that for an 18-foot tipi the poles should be about 24 or 25 feet long; they don't all have to be exactly the same length. While the lengths can vary, try not to get them shorter than 24 feet. It does not really matter what type of tree you use, although some wood is heavier than others and some is straighter. Cedar and pine were probably our best bet, for they grow very straight, are light, and there are a lot around. You can do what one of us did and just hike around in the woods until you come across trees that look good. When he found a good tree, he just cut it down. The poles you choose, when finished smooth, should be about 3 or 4 inches in diameter at the bottom and about 2 inches wide at the top where they cross. The two smoke-flap poles should be much thinner, for they don't really support the main structure. Be sure to choose the trees slightly thicker than the needed diameter to allow for shrinkage and for the loss of the bark, which has to be peeled off.

The best time to look for tree poles is in the spring when the juices are running through the inner bark. This makes the job of removing the bark much easier than at other times of the year. You should pick only young live trees, for dead trees usually have worm holes and other imperfections in them.

As you find right-on-looking trees, look at them from all angles to be sure that they are really straight. It may take a while to learn to estimate the height of trees and if they are straight or not, but every tree we thought was the right height just happened to be the right size. Maybe that was because we had seen Darry Wood's poles for his tipis lying around, leaning against trees. Trees that are about the right thickness you need are also about the right height. We used an axe at first, but it broke so the rest of the time we used a saw. After felling a tree, the first thing to do is to remove all the branches from it to make it easier to carry to where you are going to strip it. Also sharpen the butt end of the tree with an axe so that you can force the poles into the ground when the tipi is set up. If your cover seems too short you can adjust by pushing your butt points further into the ground after the tipi is up. (It should clear the ground by an inch or two everywhere except just in front.) You can also cut it off. Because your poles are long, it is a good idea to look for trees close to where your tipi will be, if possible, because it is hard to transport 25-foot poles any distance through the woods or even along a road, as one of us had to.

You should strip the poles as soon after felling them as possible. Strip them in a fairly open place so that it is easier to maneuver them. Lay a pole on two sawhorses (or something similar), hammer two large nails in each sawhorse, about 3 inches apart in one and 5 inches apart in the other, and have them stick up about 4 inches. This makes it easier to keep the poles in place while you strip them.

To strip the bark off the tree, use either a draw knife (a two-handled

25.

carpenter's tool) or a meat cleaver. We
were never able to get our hands on a draw
knife. One of our mothers suggested using
the meat cleaver and when we tried it, it
worked real well. Whatever you use, it
should be very sharp, and you will probably
have to sharpen it after every tree or two.
Strip the bark off with the knife or cleaver,
being careful, and using strokes that go
from bottom of tree to top with the grain
of the wood. Be sure to get all the bark
and inner bark off, so you get all the way
down to the real wood. If you leave any
inner bark, it tends to grow mold on it,
which doesn't look good. It's pretty
startling after a rain to go out and find that
some of your poles have turned completely
green. If your poles mildew in wet weather,
rub them with Clorox, full strength.

26.

After you have stripped all the bark
off, you must remove all the knots by level-
ing them down to the rest of the wood.
For this, use either a very sharp axe or
your meat cleaver. Sand knots down so that
the entire pole is smooth and straight. Lean
the poles up against a tree or other support,

153

and let them season in the sun for about three weeks. It is a good idea to paint the finished poles with canvas waterproofing paint (sold at camping or hardware stores) to keep them from rotting. Do this after you have finished all of your poles. One gallon is enough to give one set of poles one heavy coat and one light coat, and there should be enough left over to waterproof your pegs, too. Use any cloth rag and slop it on the poles. Don't use creosote on the poles, because it rots the canvas.

If you can't find trees for poles, some tipi manufacturers make them. But these are usually quite expensive and will drip all over when it rains, because they come in sections that must be assembled like a typical tent pole, and when it rains water will drip at the joints rather than run the length of the pole and into the ground. If you can, make the poles yourself; if you can't, buy the best two-by-fours with almost no knots. But this, of course, is not very Indian-like.

PITCHING THE TIPI

Before building your tipi, you should consider where you are going to put it when it is finished. Ideally, as we said before, the tipi should be in a field far away from any trees. If it is situated under a tree, and rainwater drips on it after the rain has stopped, mildew will form on the cover, causing dampness inside the shaded tipi, and the sun cannot dry it out. (Should this happen, use Canvak—rub it on with a rag.) Also, falling branches can puncture the cover. Because we had to use someone else's land, we got permission to use a little corner of a field. There were a few trees around so we got permission to chop off overhanging branches of the nearest trees.

Plains Indians have traditionally faced their tipis east, partly because of their religion and also because of wind directions. Because of the way a tipi is built, a wind blowing toward the door forces the smoke from the fire back down into the tipi, causing problems. The winds in inland America seldom blow from east to west, so an east-facing tipi is often best. Consider the direction your tipi will face when choosing your spot. The tipi should if possible be close to some clean water source, most likely a stream or lake. It shouldn't be too close, though—say, not closer than 100 feet, because water is home for bugs and mosquitoes. Also your tipi could be washed away in a flash flood. There was a stream about three minutes away from our site, and five gallons of water lasted the two of us for about three days.

To clear the space where your tipi will go, first get a piece of string a foot or two longer than the radius of your tipi. Drive a stake into the ground at the center of your spot. Tie the string to it and mark a circle as far as the string will reach. This is the area you will have to clear. First, get rid of all the shrubs and then rake. Clear out all the rocks and roots, so that it is pretty level. You can leave the grass for a cushion. Try and find a space relatively flat with no bumps or holes. If you don't, you'll see why after you have spent your first night there.

Now, of course, you will probably want to make a fireplace. It should go slightly toward the front of the tipi's center. This allows more room for living in the back, where you will be most of the time. The fireplace should be dug into the ground a few inches and shouldn't be too big—about 2 feet across. A good trick we learned from a friend of ours is to run a gutter pipe a few inches under the ground from the inside of the fireplace to a few feet outside the circle you have cleared. Here, on the outside end, put on a curved attachment so that it sticks up out of the ground. Put another curve on this, so that when it rains water will not get into the pipe (Fig. 27). This creates a draft and the fireplace burns better, which is very helpful, especially in the winter when your tipi will be closed up most of the time and not much extra oxygen will be able to flow into it from the outside.

27.

drainpipe for fire draft

Pitching the tipi will only require about two people, but the more the better. No tools will be necessary except maybe a measuring tape and a pencil. The first thing to do is mark off a circle around your original center point, the same diameter as that of your tipi. This will guide you in putting down the poles. For the main tripod of poles, pick out your three heaviest and strongest poles. Measuring from the bottom up (beginning <u>above</u> the butt points), mark off the distance from the edge of your tipi cover to the corner where the tie-flaps are on one of your poles (Fig. 28). Again from the bottom up, mark off the distance from the middle of the arc to the center where the tie-flaps are on your second and third poles (Fig. 28). (The distance measured on these poles should be shorter than the distance measured on the door pole.) Mark off these lengths with notches. Lay the poles on the ground as in Figure 29, having them cross on the notches you have drawn. Bind them in a clove hitch with your 1/2-inch ma-

nila rope. A clove hitch is the easiest and most practical way to tie them together (see Fig. 29). Don't cut it! Wrap the rope around the poles a few more times tightly and tie that with a square knot. The door pole has to be on the east side of the circle (or, anyway, the front—if your front door doesn't face east). So to set up the tripod, put the butt of the door pole at the east side of the circle and pull the butts of the other two down to a position where they more or less balance, on the south side. By having someone pull on the rope and someone lift the poles, it should not be too hard to get the poles upright. After this, pull out the inside pole of the two that are next to each other, and bring it over to the north side of the circle, toward the person who is holding the rope. This will form your tripod. Now space the poles evenly apart, making sure not to move the door pole. Your tripod should look like the one in Figure 30.

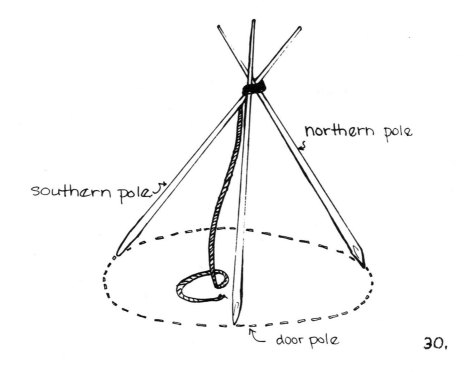

southern pole

northern pole

door pole

30.

Now lay the rest of the poles on the tripod consecutively according to the plan in Figure 31. Lay the first four "A" poles (A1, A2, A3, A4) in the FRONT CROTCH of the tripod. Lay the next four "B" poles (B5, B6, B7, B8) consecutively ON TOP OF the first set of "A" poles, also in the front crotch. Now place poles 9, 10, and 11 in the places indicated in Figure 31 and lay them in the rear crotch. Do not put up the lifting pole yet (this is the pole that will lift your cover). Wrap the rope around the poles starting at pole "S". Walk to the left pulling the rope tight. Wrap it around tight four or five times and then bring the rope down over pole "N". Let the rope hang straight down. Now drive your anchor peg in. It should be placed right next to the fireplace toward the back. Drive it in at a 45-degree angle. You can also use two pegs if you like. Drive them both in at 45-degree angles so that they cross each other. Tie the rope tightly around the pegs. You are now ready to start on the cover.

Pole Sequence

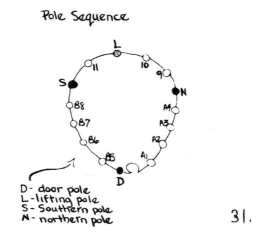

D - door pole
L - lifting pole
S - Southern pole
N - northern pole

31.

32. Looking up through poles

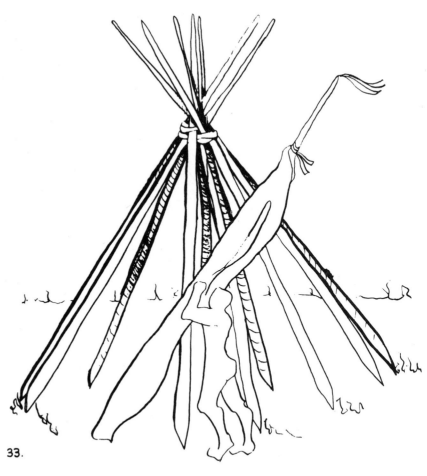

33.

PUTTING UP THE COVER

Lay the cover down on the ground with the outside showing, slip the last pole you have left under it so that it is aligned with the center mark down the middle of the cover. Tie the tie-tapes around the pole very tightly so that they won't slip. Fold the corner of one side over to the center where pole is. Do the same with the opposite corner. Continue this pattern until the cover is folded up into two rolls. Pick up the pole and the cover and lift it into position. It will be obvious where it has to be laid, with the cover on the outside. Now it is a simple matter to unroll each roll around the frame. Find a sturdy stick about 4 feet long and tie tightly horizontally across the two front poles, one being the door-pole, about 5 feet from the ground. By standing on this stick, it should not be difficult to tie the smoke-flap tapes and insert the top lacing pins. While you are up there, get someone to help you fit the smoke-flap poles into the pockets of the smoke flaps. It will be quite difficult to do if you don't do it now. If you don't expect cold

158

34.

weather or rain, you'll sometimes want to pull the lower corners of the smoke-flaps back against the tipi or attach them to poles a short distance from the door, depending on the ventilation you want to get (Fig. 35). So tie ropes through each buttonhole now. Take down the stick and finish lac-

35. Smoke-flaps and
the door open for
maximum ventilation

ing the cover down. The cover will probably fit loosely around the frame so go inside and push out all the poles an equal amount to make the cover fit tightly. Now you have to peg down the cover.

PEGGING DOWN THE COVER

The idea is to space pegs attached by ropes to the canvas evenly all around the tipi. Have two pegs by the door. To attach the 20-25 pegs to the cover of our 18-foot tipi, you will need as many 3/4-inch marbles or round rocks as you have pegs. You will also need the same number of 2 1/2-to- 3-foot lengths of 1/4-inch nylon cord. Hold each marble on the inside of the cover a few inches from the bottom. Tie a length of cord around the marble from the outside with a square knot. Make sure to have an equal amount of cord left on both sides of the knot. Tie the two ends around the top of a peg. Twist the peg until the cord is tight. Then drive the peg into the ground, tilting it away from the tipi. Do this with all the pegs all around the cover. Watch out for rocks in the ground. A really good idea is to drive an iron stake first in the place where you will drive your peg, so that you won't ruin the peg.

36. Cover peg in position

HANGING THE LINING

Now that you have finished with the cover, you can start on the lining. For this you will need a long length of cotton cord or clothesline. Tie one end to the lifting pole about 6 feet from the ground. You start from the lifting pole so that if for some reason you have to take down the cover, you won't also have to take down the lining. Bring the cord across the pole next to the lifting pole and around it. Bring the cord across the next pole. You have a loop around the first pole. Continue to do this all around the tipi, making sure to keep the rope 6 feet above the ground. When you have gone all the way around, go around the whole thing again. Go around to each pole and pull the rope as tight as you can. Now tie the end of the rope to the last pole next to the lifting pole. Go around to each pole and shove two 2-to-5-inch-long sticks in each loop around the poles. Space the sticks about 2 inches apart on the side of the pole facing toward the center of the tipi. This will keep water running down the poles from running off down the rope for the pegs provide a channel for water to go. Now take the four-paneled piece of lining and the 6-inch tie-tapes you cut and tie the middle buttonholes to the rope right next to the lifting pole. Take the next tie-tape and tie that to the cord, and so on until the whole piece is up. Now take a three-paneled piece and tie one end to the cord next to the door. Tie the next tie-tape to where it reaches, working your way to the back of the tipi. Do the same with the other three-paneled piece. The pieces should overlap each other some. From the outside, pull the bottom of the lining so that there's no sagging and pull it back in the direction of the cover. Put a rock on top of the lining where it touches the ground. Do this all around, and use plenty of rocks. Every now and then you will have to go around and pull the lining back a little. The rocks sometimes tend to slip.

Small sticks between rope and pole make a channel for water.

38.

37.

the lining

FINISHING UP

There is one more thing you have to do. Dig a trench all around the outside of the tipi a few inches out from the base of the poles. Also, dig a run-off channel at the lowest point of the trench. The trench should be 3 or 4 inches wide and 3 or 4 inches deep. After a few rains, you will have to redig the trench because it tends to shallow out. This trench is quite necessary, especially if you are situated near a hill. It keeps water from running through and swamping the middle of your tipi when it's raining.

Depending on the type of lining you make for your tipi, there are many different kinds of floor you can use. The Plains Indians used a layer or two of animal hides for rugs and, as the bottom ones wasted away from dampness or use, just replaced them with no trouble. Today, animal hides are not as easy to come by. In our tipi we have burlap around the fire-place so that any rain that might happen to find its way into our tipi will run through the burlap into the ground. A couple of feet away from the center we have a waterproof tarp all around and then rugs on top of that, except in front of the door. We find this is a realistic floor layout. Paul's mother gave us a rug she wasn't using and Steve's mother gave us a few she didn't want. A friend just found a perfectly good rug at the town dump for his tent. Don't take good rugs into your tent until the ground gets really dry, or you will have moldy rugs. The first time we put up our tipi we had a plastic tarp covering the whole floor with a hole in it for the fireplace. The plastic tarp reached out to the edge of the tipi and was tucked under the lining. Water that came off the outside of the tipi lining dripped on the plastic. That night it rained and we found out why this is not a good thing to do—we were soaked! Water came in from all over. If you plan on living in your tipi permanently, you might want to build it on a wooden floor. You can use plywood, although a friend of ours says that plywood warps. He recommends using floor boards. If you build a wooden floor, build it above

39. Darry Wood and
Barbara Wood
making a tipi floor

the ground a few inches to avoid unnecessary dampness, and for insulation. You can even use linoleum; that reminds us too much of kitchens, but okay if you don't have anything else! If you are traveling light with your tipi, don't use anything.

A sleeping bag and maybe a small foam mat under it is all you really need to sleep in. Anything else just winds up getting dirty. If you are living in your tipi, you will probably sleep under blankets instead of a sleeping bag, so have anyone who comes in remove their shoes. Tipis can get dirty in just one day. Always have a small broom around. It comes in handy.

BUILDING A FIRE

It will probably take you a while to learn how to build a decent fire unless you are really an experienced camper. I guess we're not. I believe we smoked ourselves out three times our first night. First rule of the tipi fire: don't build big fires. Second rule: never let the fire smolder or go out, or at least not until you know what you're doing. If you get the fire going right, there is nothing like sitting around the fire at night. When you're building fires in a tipi, you have to watch out what kind of wood you use. Don't use any kind of pine, as it throws live sparks that burn large holes in whatever they happen to land on. Try not to burn too much green wood either. It makes a lot of smoke. Probably oak or maple are the best woods to use. They're good hard wood, burn slowly, and don't throw sparks. Dried-out pine twigs are great for kindling, but not for firewood.

TIPS

If you take proper care of your tipi, it should last eight or ten years. If your tipi will be exposed to the weather all year around, there are some basic maintenance rules to remember. In the winter after a snow, check your cover and clear away any snow banked up around the outside. Be sure to clear all the way down to the base of the tipi. You must do this because air might get in under the cover to create an unwanted draft on the fire. It is a good idea to get all the snow off the entire cover to insure long life for the canvas. Your fire will melt any snow above the level of the lining, so don't worry about the top half. Most people find that it helps to build some sort of wind-breaker around the tipi to keep cold drafts from blowing under the cover. It shouldn't be too hard to make one out of hay. If you are planning on living in your tipi during the winter months, be sure to have a lot of wood stored up, for you will be having your fire going all day long. A friend of ours made a wooden walk leading over the field to his tipi. It was easy to shovel in the winter, also when it is muddy it's good to walk on.

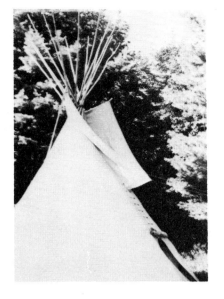

40.

For cooking, you can use a small Colman stove, but you don't need it. We have found that you can cook anything over the fire just as well as over a stove. You can bake, fry, broil, grill, or just heat up things. You can even toast bread by putting a slice on a stick and holding it over the fire. Any camping book will tell you how to do this. At first we had a small stove, but we haven't used it for months. Cooking over the fire is almost easier, and much cheaper too.

The Indians had their special ways of cooking. To boil water they heated rocks red-hot over fire and then dropped them in water, and instantly the water was boiling. To cook things, they dug a pit and lined it with rocks. Then they built a fire in it. After the rocks had heated sufficiently, they cleaned out the coals and put a buffalo skin over the rocks. Then the food was put in and covered. They also cooked things over the fire. Many Indians made jerky, which is strips of dried-out meat. The strips could be stored almost indefinitely if they were not subjected to dampness. The jerky could be eaten straight or boiled in water to regain its tenderness.

If you are going to leave your camp overnight or longer, make your food inaccessible to animals. Put it in a sack and hang it 4 or 5 feet from the ground on the rope hanging from the top of your tipi. If you don't do this, when you come back bring more food and something to clean up with. Raccoons have a habit of making an awful mess out of any food they can get their hands on. This has happened to us many times. Sometimes they will just take one thing and eat it outside, but most of the time they will eat it inside. One time we came back to our tipi and found oats, powdered milk, and flour all over the floor. We also found little raisin skins scattered about.

We have always worried about someone stumbling on our tipi and slashing the canvas, but no one ever has. Once when we went to take the tipi down from Steve's house to Paul's we found some beer cans, broken bottles, plastic spoons, and .22 cartridges lying around. Obviously some hunters had used the tipi. That is one reason to have the tipi near your house if you're not going to be actively living in it.

A survival book that helped us a lot was The Golden Book of Camping, published around 1940. It was corny-looking, but the contents turned out to be helpful.

Did it ever occur to you how the Indians and other people living in the elements dealt with the elementary problem of building a john? Along with Fire, Water, and Air, you need to dig out a latrine at least a hundred yards away. Keep a shovel handy. Cover up and dig another one every couple of weeks. We made a seat out of a split log with each half resting on rocks. Latrines should be far away because of bugs.

Well, that's about all we can tell you. We hope that you have as much fun in your tipi as we have had in ours. Good luck, and keep a stiff upper lip.

Stephen Halogh   *Paul Alexander*

Video
Making Media

True Light Beavers / Tobe Carey

When's the last time you turned on your TV set and liked what you saw? When's the last time you thought the show you were watching had any relationship to reality? When's the last time you were really happy watching TV?

Today there are people working with inexpensive video equipment who are committed to making strong personal statements on television. You can join their underground ranks easily.

The new video movement has spread rapidly across the North American continent, and has turned on numbers of people who had never thought they could influence TV programming, never mind create their own shows. These video groups, widespread in both urban and rural areas, are the vanguard of the electronic revolution. With their own or borrowed equipment they are producing significant programming for both regional and national audiences.

Many video groups live collectively and share their equipment and editing facilities. They strive to involve their local community and to turn on individuals to the potential in video tape. They regularly demonstrate the equipment to the community, and give people the opportunity to try their hands at producing TV. It's truly giving media-power to the people.

And the fact is that there is nothing mysterious about television. There is no shrouded secret about techniques behind the shows that reach you through your television set. All you need to know about basic television production can be absorbed in a few hours of using video-tape equipment. After a demonstration, people are much more aware of what they are watching on TV, and can better discriminate between shows. Visual literacy is an important attribute for anyone living in twentieth-century America.

Since the inception of half-inch video format there has been a problem in getting completed tapes viewed by audiences. One major hang-up is the unwillingness of the high-powered broadcasting industry to consider using half-inch tapes for its productions. They claim half-inch standards aren't rigid enough and the on-the-air quality leaves much to be desired. But it seems as though what they are really concerned about is keeping the doors to broadcast facilities effectively closed to those without broadcast-approved union cards. In effect, they are maintaining a monopoly on the television system, keeping it in the hands of the big money people. It simply costs too much to equip a two-inch or even a one-inch television production facility that can produce what THEY have determined to be the standards of the industry. To further complicate matters, they cloak their reluctance to use half-inch video in Federal Communications Commission regulations, insisting on engineering standards that don't apply and serve to effectively bar the new video from being broadcast.

In the disastrous 1972 floods in the Wilkes-Barre area of Pennsylvania, one local-broadcast TV station lost all its cameras and "professional" studio equipment. They did, however, salvage their transmitter and antenna system. All they needed was cameras and video-tape recorders to get back on the air. Then local high-school students came by with half-inch equipment and offered it to provide emergency coverage of flood conditions and relief efforts. The station, having no alternative, took the half-inch equipment and went back on the air. The signals went out over their regular broadcast channel with excellent results. The point is, once the effort is made, the engineers can successfully broadcast half-inch video over existing transmitting facilities.

Fortunately, while this has been happening, the burgeoning cable systems have begun to play more and more half-inch tape. They are able to connect half-inch equipment directly into their local-origination cables, and to push the signal out with at least as good quality as signals captured either off the air from broadcast stations or from their own one-inch production facilities. This has opened new opportunities for half-inch productions to be seen by relatively wide audiences.

I have produced shows on half-inch video for Cablevision, Kingston, N.Y., and, with few exceptions, the quality has held up extremely well. There seems to be no excuse for excluding half-inch from a share of the video market (no reason other than the rigidity of the broadcast industry).

Other distribution outlets have begun to open in the last few years. One alternative has been the video-access banks managed by alternative video groups such as Raindance (New York), Johnny Video Tape (California), Intermedia (Canada), Media Access (California), Videfreex (New York), and Community Video Center (Washington, D.C.). These groups collect and swap or sell software (tapes) for individuals and groups. Check them for details.

Other outlets are growing on the college and high-school campuses. Many schools already have their own half-inch equipment and are using it to show prepackaged materials. Much of this programming is coming from lecture bureaus—commercial agencies that make money by packaging a whole documentary-type show. They are trying to promote and tap the commercial potential of the half-inch video field. The bureaus are developing programming that is sometimes interesting, since it takes advantage of video's ability to present uncensored material.

There are also a number of video theaters springing up. Located mostly in urban areas, they provide yet another source for software distribution. Often they are linked with the prepackaging people, but sometimes they can be persuaded to show what you have produced. Already such theaters are in operation in New York, Boston, San Francisco, Chicago, etc. Check local entertainment sheets for specifics on this changing scene.

Along with the collective video groups that are spreading the word and producing low-cost television, there are individual artists working personally within the medium. Many of them have been turned on to video tape by seeing their work immediately after recording it. Many former filmmakers have switched to the video medium because of this important capability of video tape.

My own background in media stems from film, and now embraces both film and video. And it was the instant-replay quality of video, the considerably shortened time between shooting and editing, that first attracted me. No longer do I have to wait for film to be sent to a lab, to be processed, to be sent back, before I can start editing. No longer do I have to work with silent footage while composing a film. (The sound's already there.) Now I can have the video tape completely shot and ready for viewing in the literal flick of a switch.

The video process is exciting and immediate. In McLuhanesque terms, it is involving and personal. It is, as any TV freak can tell you, a totally absorbing medium, one that sucks you into its grip almost without your knowing it.

This makes it all the more important that people become aware of its power and equally aware of how they can add their vision to it. Personal and collective statements belong on television, and individuals and groups beholden to no broadcast power-system must be encouraged to produce television shows that will reveal the true character of America.

BASIC EQUIPMENT

Video tape is the thing that television is made of. And, due to recent innovations in the field of camera and recorder/playback design, television can now be made in the home.

The minimal equipment needed for recording and playing back your own television shows is a camera with a video-tape recorder capable of recording and playing back through an ordinary TV set. There are a growing number of available video outfits on the market, such as Sony, Ampex, Panasonic, Craig, Toshiba, and AKAI. All the above make video units that use half-inch tape format, with the exception of AKAI, which uses a smaller, quarter-inch tape size. (It's really unclear yet whether there is an advantage in half-inch over quarter-inch, or vice versa. Time and experience will tell.) All of these units are considerably cheaper and less sophisticated than the "professional" one-inch and two-inch video-tape machines used by TV stations. They offer greater portability and savings in tape costs, while providing a picture and sound whose quality rivals some of the larger units.

As the video movement has developed, and as the hardware (equipment) has improved, individuals and groups have chosen their units on the basis of versatility. In this chapter I emphasize the Sony AV 3400 VideoRover II (Portapak) as the standard recording equipment, since it is the most popular recorder in use, and still seems to offer the best in portable recording AND playback capabilities.

Portapak and monitor set-up

When you get access to a portable video-tape recorder (VTR) and camera, you will be able to record on a roll of tape up to a half-hour of synchronous-sound (meaning, when the lips move, the words come out) black-and-white video tape. Also, you can usually play back the tape on the same machine, viewing through the camera viewfinder (actually a miniature TV set), and listening through a small earphone.

The units will function either on AC-110 house current or on an enclosed rechargeable battery. The battery may provide as much as 45 minutes of running time on a 6-10 hour recharging time. However, some batteries have been known to give out in as little as twenty minutes, so be sure to know what your system is capable of doing.

Part of making video is getting the chance to show it off. To do this, using the portable units, you have to get an RF adaptor that plugs into the bottom of the unit. This converts the video output of the VTR to a broadcast frequency that can be picked up by a television set tuned to the channel corresponding to the RF unit used. The RF unit is connected from the VTR to the TV set by two leads which attach to the antenna terminals. Nothing could be simpler to hook up.

With this equipment, you are set to record and play back video tapes.

A word about technical information: The instruction manuals that come with the equipment are fairly clear and straightforward. All the basic stuff about handling the equipment is in the manual. Be sure to read it through before you go off shooting.

A final equipment note: as far as I know, all half-inch gear now being manufactured meets standard industry specifications. Most brands are now compatible with one another. The system used is called the EIAJ-1 standard. All Sony equipment with an AV prefix meets this standard. Any equipment you run across with a CV designation does NOT meet this standard. Sometimes the older CV equipment is offered on sale—don't get it, because it won't fit standard equipment. Whenever you buy used equipment, make sure you get some kind of guarantee, as a lot of equipment is on the market because it's broken down. (There is an adaptor called an octopus cable that can be used to convert CV signal to AV equipment.)

HOW IT WORKS

In the video-tape system the image received by the camera is converted into a series of electrical impulses that are fed to the video-tape recorder.

The record head receives the impulses and, as the half-inch magnetic tape (similar to quarter-inch sound recording tape) passes over it, the impulses alter the polarity of the iron oxide coating on the tape. When the tape is played back, the VTR receives a weak electrical current from the altered polarity pattern on the recorded tape. This current re-creates the pattern received originally by the VTR from the camera, and makes the images you see on the TV screen.

LENSES

The fine thing about video-taping is not having to wait for the developer—you can see what you are recording right as you record it. You really don't have to be hip to all the technical details of lenses. If things look weird on the monitor screen while you're recording, all you have to do is find the controls and do a little experimenting. Or take another look at your instruction book.

The 12.5-50 mm. zoom lens provided with the portable camera is sufficient to use outdoors under daylight conditions, and indoors with adequate light. The lens has an adjustable focal length (the longer the focal length, the smaller the area of the subject that will be seen, but the more it will be magnified). When the lens is at the wide-angle position (12.5 mm.) the field of view will be larger than normal (25 mm.). This lens position tends to distort the image some. In close-up, telephoto position (35-50 mm.) the perspective will appear flattened in the scene.

With portable VTR cameras you can change lenses. The camera accepts all lenses with a screw-type C-mount. Most 16-mm. film cameras accept this same type of lens. They can be used from an extremely wide angle (8 mm.) to a very long one (1000 mm.). When using long lenses (or when the zoom lens is in the 50 mm. position) you must be careful not to jar the camera. If you do, the image will jump much more noticeably than if you were using a lens of a shorter focal length. Tripods and monopods are very helpful to steady the camera.

Since the video system requires adequate light to record a decent image, you must be sure that your lens allows enough light to pass through it. This means being sure that your lens iris (the adjustable opening in the lens that lets the light through) is opened to the correct place. This means checking the F-stop (the numbers on the lens barrel nearest the camera).

The F-stops range from 1.8 (wide open) to 22 (closed down). Each time you turn to a higher number, the light passing through the iris is cut in half. You can visually check whether or not you have enough light to shoot by placing the VTR in record mode, removing the lens cap from the camera, and looking into the small viewfinder/monitor. If the image looks sharp and the blacks and whites look clear, then the signal being received by the camera is good. If things look gray and dim, check to see that your lens is opened to the correct F-stop. Chances are that most of your taping will be done at F-1.8. Experience has shown that this opening generally gives "correct" pictures.

FOCUSING

A note on focusing: when using a zoom lens, always focus on your object with the lens at its longest focal length (50 mm.). Once in focus at this point, it will remain in focus throughout the zoom range (as long as you don't shift the camera to another position). By watching your image in the camera viewfinder, you can see if you have a correct focus. This will be very clear in a close-up (telephoto position) but much less clear in a wide-angle shot. So, be sure you are in correct focus before you zoom back to a wide-angle shot.

THE CABLE

The camera is connected to the portable VTR by a length of gray cable. For some obscure reason, they've made the cable just long enough to trip on, and just short enough to make you nearly immobile. Wherever you go, the VTR must follow. This is O.K. when you feel like carrying it, but there are other occasions when an extra length of cable would be helpful. Fortunately, there are extensions available from all the manufacturers (at an extra charge).

LIGHTS

If you aren't prepared beforehand, lights for indoor taping can be a problem. Should friends call and say to hurry over with the Portapak and catch the baby as she plays on the rug, first ask about the lighting. If they're not sure, bring along your own.

There are many high-powered quartz lights available for video and film work that are excellent. Usually they come rated at 600 watts or 1000 watts, and one light is often adequate to flood smallish rooms in homes. To tape in larger spaces, you will want to add still more lights, and then I recommend following the standard three-light set-up preferred by most professionals (see diagram below). Light stands and clamps are available from manufacturers (Colotran-G.B.C. and Lowell-Lite).

If quartz lights are not available or outside your budget, think about spots and floods that can be bought from the closest hardware store. Most hardware outlets will also carry hand clamps and reflectors that can house the 150-watt or 200-watt bulbs. Photography stores are another good source for these lights and clamps. Don't forget to get enough extension cords.

If you can't get any of these lights, try ordinary lamps and put aluminum foil inside the shades to reflect the light. Or you can put aluminum foil in flat sheets on cardboard or make a cone shape to direct the light a bit. Experiment around.

ONE CAUTION ABOUT LIGHTS: Never point the video camera directly into any bright light source (lamp or sun). The light will mar the delicate vidicon tube with sometimes a permanent "burn," which will appear as a dark line on the video image. Cost to replace: $85.

Lighting set-up for action. The subject is moving from right to left, with the camera following in a panning movement. Each half of the lighting set-up can be considered a standard three-light set-up.

When a subject will be moving, you must cover the area into which it will move. In the diagram above, use is made of strong key lights (spotlights) for casting shadows, floodlights to illuminate the general area of the scene, and back lights, which aid in clarifying the subject from the background. All the lights are aimed down on the subject from a 45-degree angle in order to closely approximate natural lighting. For a scene in which there is no movement, the basic three-light set-up (see above) provides ample lighting. In cases where you have to rely on less than three lights, be sure that enough illumination is on the section of the scene where you expect most of the action to occur.

MIKES AND SOUND

Most half-inch systems have a built-in omnidirectional mike (I'll explain this in a minute) just above the lens. This allows you to work the entire unit by yourself, and makes for nice personal video. But the quality of the sound you will get leaves something to be desired. In a small room with just a few folks it'll be OK. But outdoors, or in a large gathering, the VTR's Automatic Gain Control (AGC) will seek the loudest sound and adjust the recording level to receive that sound (and oftentimes that particular sound is not the one you want to emphasize on your tape). This sound problem came home to me very acutely when I was doing a tape of a childbirth in Mexico. The house in which the birth was taking place was situated on the Yucatan Peninsula, right on the Caribbean Sea. The night of the delivery, a storm was blowing up, and the waves were loud and clear in the room. The VTR picked up this sound of wind and waves as the loudest general sound and, throughout much of the beginning portion of the tape, these relatively unimportant sounds were muffling the conversation between the people involved in helping with the birth.

So you may want to supplement the built-in mike (which also picks up mechanical clicks from the zooming of the lens) with an external mike that can get close to your subject. Fortunately, most systems provide an exterior mike input, or jack. What you will need is an auxiliary mike with a mini-plug. Or, if you want, you can deploy several mikes and run them through a sound mixer to combine the sound of one or more mikes before they get to the VTR. The mixer in use, however, must provide a mike output, or the audio signal will overload the circuit of the VTR.

There are several kinds of mike to choose from and, without getting into a course on sound, a few differences bear mentioning.

Omnidirectional: these mikes accept sound from all directions. They are useful for getting the feeling of a crowd scene, a rock or folk group, or in other situations where a number of people are involved.

Unidirectional: these tend to emphasize sounds coming from the front of the microphone and are useful to control (decrease) sounds that might otherwise impinge on the recording. Shotgun mikes are an extension of this idea, and some sophisticated ones (Sennheiser's, for example) are particularly good in candid work. They allow the sound-man to remain quite far from the subject while still picking up and getting a good recording.

All mikes should have about 15 to 20 feet of cord attached for greatest mobility. The more independent the sound and camera, the more versatile the taping situation can become. Of course using an external mike means using a sound-man or -woman.

The sound-person should be supplied with a good set of earphones that can also be jacked into the VTR. Using the small plastic earpiece that comes with the set is really not adequate for determining how good the sound is.

Most half-inch systems allow for the addition of a separate voice track. You can dub (add a sound track without erasing the visual track) while playing back the prerecorded tape. It is a form of editing.

EDITING

Many people like to record things they see and leave them unchanged. They are not interested in altering the dynamics of a situation through editing. For recordings like that, the portable video systems serve well.

But for those interested in building on, adding to, and/or dramatizing their original recorded material, editing is a must. In addition to all the currently designed portable video equipment, you need an editing deck to edit. That also means cables and wires connecting it to the VTR deck and monitors on which to view the editing. A monitor is a TV receiver that can take a signal (picture and audio) directly from the video-tape recorder by way of a connecting cable. Most monitors can be used like an ordinary TV set.

The original recording (also called "original," "master," and "first generation") is never physically cut when you use this electronic editing system. This is a major difference between film and video tape. In video there is much less handling of the basic material, the tape. Although the images may be compared to frames, unlike film they cannot be looked at with the human eye alone for visual information.

RF unit cable

monitor

monitor

Monitor cable

Dubbing cable

AV 3400

MASTER (Original)

AV 3650

SLAVE (Editing deck)

In a simple editing set-up, the original taped footage is copied by the slave unit in an edited sequence. You may build on this system, adding new sounds and more visuals to already collected materials. A key to the operation is timing and you may want to invest in a stopwatch.

The copy ("second generation," "slave") when completed will be an edited tape, ready for viewing by an audience. The editing process allows you to add sound and to change the sequence of material. It also allows you to shorten sequences for dramatic or other effects. And it allows you to add material from more than one reel of tape to the composite (edited) copy.

Most editing of half-inch video tape is done by matching master-slave tapes on two VTR systems, either Portapak to editing deck or editing deck to editing deck, and watching both tapes on TV monitors attached to the video sources. When you see the picture you want on monitor #1, you hit the edit button on the editing deck, which duplicates the signal on the slave tape and monitor #2.

There are a number of home-grown systems for editing being developed as people get more familiar with the available equipment. The Sony and Panasonic editing decks have a built-in editing function that can give rock-solid edits when things work just right. The problem is to get the correct edit points in synchronous line-up on the two machines. If the counter on the portable unit turned at the same speed as the counter on the editing deck, it would solve some problems. As it is, you'll probably want to develop your own system for achieving effective synchronization after some experimentation.

Some systems already in use involve marking X's with felt-tip pens on the tape itself, and lining up these spots with the skew bar (first post after the supply reel on the VTR). This is one system that sounds complicated on paper, but when shown by someone using the method is quite simple. Others incorporate counters that have been added to the machines, which allow the editor to get both edit points in line and then back off a given amount of numerals, to begin the warm-up or the "roll-in." Once you have the exact beginning of the section to be added ready for playing, and the exact end of the previously edited section ready to be added to, you must back up enough to allow the two machines to lock up in sync (synchronization: signals that lock the horizontal and vertical scanning in step; if sync is off the picture will roll or flutter). This means that both machines need ample run-in time before the actual edit is made. If they don't have adequate lead-in, the edit will be unstable, and the jump from sequence to sequence will be noticeable on the edited tape.

The key is to move both supply reels of tape back far enough to allow for proper roll-in, while ensuring that the original tape reaches the playback head of its VTR at the same time that the second-generation tape reaches the record head of the editing deck. When you know your machines well, you may be able to do this simply by counting the number of turns you have to make on both supply reels. Or you can use a measuring device that fits on the reels. This tells you how many revolutions you need to have the scenes in sync.

As I said, one key to editing is accessibility to two monitors: one for the output of the master tape and the other for the output of the edited version. This will allow you to see and hear the editing points on the two tapes as they reach the critical places. If the edit looks like it'll be all right, punch up the edit button at the proper moment, and you should have a suitable edit.

Playing back an edited tape should be done on an editing deck. If you try to play back an edited tape on the portable unit you will again see the edit points as they roll by. This is simply because the playback mechanism in the portable VTR is not up to handling the impulses from the edit points. There are several proven techniques that may be of use in editing collected material. When contrasting and opposing views are placed against one another, in succession, the viewer gets a synthesis of the material that is stronger than if each scene were presented alone.

Cross-cutting can be effective to make a point, or to dramatically build towards a moment of crisis. Remember the dramatic film scenes where the heroine is tied to the railroad tracks, and the train is seen rushing towards her? The effect is heightened by showing a shot of the helpless girl, and than a separate shot of the train coming closer to the camera. The girl is then seen struggling again, and then the train looms larger. This is a classic example of cross-cutting.

Keep edited scenes to their essentials, paring back until the compiled version is sparse and taut. But you may also want to add complementary or contrasting visuals to a scene without disturbing the audio portion. Often these are cut-aways, shots of things other than the main action, that add to the viewer's interest, information, or mood.

DIRECTING

Everyone must develop her or his own way of handling video situations, but it may help you to jot down a few thoughts before beginning. The better prepared you are for any situation, the better will be your tape. But if it's not necessary to have anything like a script, you can also simply trip out on the event as it occurs.

Be aware of a few things. When taping with the portable half-inch unit, always leave ten seconds from the time you begin recording until the time

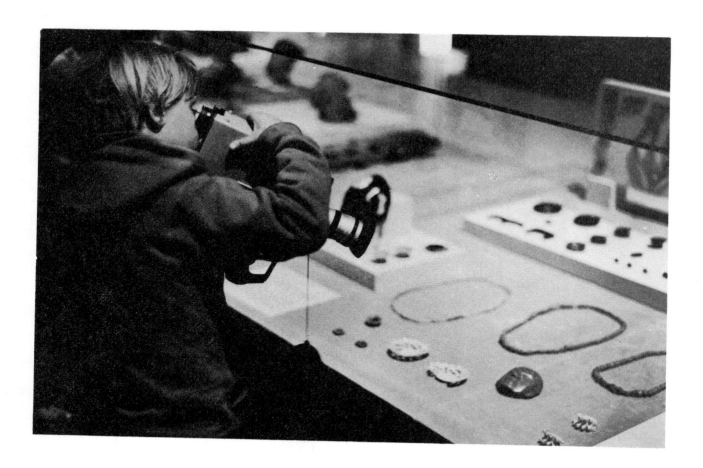

when you want your information to begin on the tape. This will allow enough time for the VTR to get up proper speed and sync. If you fail to do this, you'll have trouble making solid edits with material at the beginning of your shot.

Keep in mind that TV can give a lot of information in a short period of time, and that constant changes of the image may keep viewer interest high. On the other hand, don't keep zooming in and out or panning around without having a purpose. Every shot you make should have a reason for being on the tape; otherwise it is wasted effort.

Don't get so hung up on the synchronous sound capability that all your tapes become interview or talk shows. Use the portable nature of the camera and recorder to get into action situations.

Be aware of framing and composition. Leave anything out that is not essential to what you want to show. Be aware that camera angles can affect the way your material looks. A high angle (looking down on the subject) can make the figures less imposing, while a low angle (looking up from the floor) can make a small person look more menacing. Generally a head-on approach is comfortable for viewers, although a dramatic effect can be achieved by using other carefully chosen camera angles.

The relatively small TV screen does not show long shots well.

Long shot (L.S.)

Medium shot (M.S.)

Close up (C.U.)

These are the typical TV images:
    Long shot (l.s.)—the figure and surroundings
    Medium shot (m.s.)—head and shoulders of a person
    Close-up (c.u.)—head of a person

If you know your scene doesn't call for much action, you might want to use a tripod. It helps steady the image, and keeps viewers from feeling seasick as they watch. It's especially vital to steady large and heavy telephoto lenses—and it will give your weary hand a rest.

Don't be afraid to direct a scene to get what you want. Every piece of art has a point of view—there is no objectivity in TV—just don't claim to be objective, and your statement can stand by itself. Every video tape is automatically "exclusionary," automatically places a frame around certain objects and not others. If you want to present two sides of a story, go ahead, but remember that most stories have more than two sides—many shades of gray.

Pacing and rhythm are vital parts of any video production, be it documentary or dramatic in nature. They determine the length of each shot and the way in which shots are placed in order. Shots that last more than six or seven seconds each are relatively long, and may call for shortening in the editing process.

Keep in mind certain edits you may want as you work, and look for material that might help fill in whatever scheme comes to mind. If you have an idea beforehand of how much material you want the final tape to have, you'll know about how much you want to shoot. Video tapes can be erased and reused, so don't be afraid to shoot more than you end up using.

A good way to fantasize what you want the tape to look and sound like is to close your eyes and imagine the scenes on a TV set. That will be your visuals. Then hear the sounds in your head. That will be your audio. The next step is to try to recreate the scenes as you imagined them.

Once the material has been gathered, you will want to review it several times, jotting down notes (it's a good idea to carry a little notebook) about the tapes. The half-inch units have a counter that can be used to help locate material when the editing time comes. Simply line up your first scene and get the counter to 000. Then you're ready to log the tape, jotting down a short description of the scene and the counter number where it appears on the tape.

If you want to go beyond a simple one-camera system, you will need a few more pieces of hardware. To run more than one camera into a recording deck, you need a camera switcher (also called camera selector) and a sync generator (to keep the camera signals in line with each other) or a special effects generator (SEG), which can accept up to four cameras at once, and which will allow you to change from one signal to another while taping. This will give you the capability of covering a scene from three or four different angles at one time, and creating an edited tape by choosing your shots while the initial taping is going on.

SEG's can supply interesting visual effects.

Cut: one shot immediately replaced by another.

Fade-in: starting with a black screen, the shot is gradually brought up to full brilliance.

Fade-out: starting from a fully brilliant picture, the shot is gradually brought to black.

Split screen: two shots share the screen at the same time.

Mix (dissolve): one shot is gradually faded out while a second shot is faded in to replace it. The signals cross to make a superimposition at one point.

Superimpose: placing one shot over the other—good for titles, cut lines, etc.

Wipe: one shot pushes the other off the screen. There are several ways the wipe may enter the screen.

Note: To make fade-ins and fade-outs without using a special effects generator, you can use the F-stop ring on the lens. Simply close down the lens all the way (turn to highest F-stop number) when you begin shooting, and gradually open to the correct F-stop. That will give you a fade-in. Do the reverse (from wide-open lens to closed-down) for a fade-out.

EQUIPMENT CARE

Here are some tips:

Watch out for extremely hot or cold situations. In very bright sun or intense heat you might drape a piece of white muslin over the VTR to save the battery from being drained. I did that in Mexico, and regularly preserved the battery charge.

Keep the heads clean. The portable units come with a cleaning kit, but if the fluid runs out, pure alcohol on chamois leather will work as well. If the heads get clogged, the VTR may not record at all. (Use a demagnetizer periodically on the heads.)

The covers on the portable units have a tendency to loosen. This is especially likely to happen if you leave a unit on its side. Then, while you're taping, the cover may rub against the take-up reel and cause the tape to wind itself around nearby rollers and capstans. When this happens, the tape is like useless spaghetti and has to be cut off.

Lens tissue: be sure never to touch the lens glass with your fingers. If the lens does get dirty, use lens tissue only (not eyeglass papers—they scratch). Carry some with you and, before each taping session, check the lens for dirt. A few circular wipes with the soft tissue will prevent dirty spots from appearing on the tape.

VIDEO TO FILM

Since the number of video playback units is far less than the number of 16-mm. film projectors, you might want to think about transferring a completed video tape to film. There are outfits that will do this for you at a fairly reasonable rate, and there are also ways to do it yourself.

To have a commercially done transfer made will cost between $9 and $12 per minute of film for one composite (sound and picture) print. Some places to check for prices and quality are: Rombex Productions Corp., 245 West 55 St., New York, N.Y.; and Windsor Electronic Systems Corporation, 230-08 South Conduit Avenue, Laurelton, N.Y. 11413.

If you want to try your hand at transferring video to film, simply set up your playback deck corrected to a monitor, and begin the tape. Put your movie camera in front of the monitor, set the correct F-stop, and film away. Film speed should be comparable to the number of frames per second of video playback—about 30 frames per second. The sharpness you usually expect from a film image will, of course, be lacking in a video-film transfer. But you'll have a copy that can be shown on a projector. Needless to say, unless you have very sophisticated film equipment, you will just get the visuals without the audio. So you'll need a sound-tape-recorder running at the same time, to pick up the voice and music track. Then, when playing back the film, you'll have to use the sound tape as well.

A FEW PROJECTS

There's plenty you can do—here are some projects I've found to be good. The use to the community of half-inch video is limitless. Say you wanted to show local groups how certain industries were polluting the environment, you could really do it with video: waste going down the streams, smoke in the air, etc. Not everyone can show up at the town meetings but you could tape them for replay to community groups, schools, and cable television, which is looking and will sometimes pay for such programming.

In fact, the political uses of video tape are fantastic. Candidates can record their opinions. Talk a shopkeeper into using his shopwindow for replay, and people will stop by to listen and watch. Also you can record political rallies, speeches, and all the rest. This way both issues and candidates will get broader coverage, particularly local ones.

Every area has its special events and there isn't always a commercial operation around to record them. Last summer in nearby Phoenicia, N.Y., a group of architects got together from all over the East Coast and formed what was called "quick city": simple shelters that could be both erected and inhabited in a day. Tipis, domes, tents, plastic structures were all put up in a grassy meadow, high in the mountains. And it was great to have all this on tape. I've used it and shown it many times.

Making a permanent record of other kinds of craft is important. Somebody makes something special and then either sells or gives it away. If you have video equipment you can make a record of it, and if possible how it was made, for the use of craftspeople as well as the general public. Public libraries are showing active interest in forming a collection of video tapes and, from my experience, their initial interest has been in the crafts. The Mid-Hudson library system (Market St., Poughkeepsie, New York) has started a collection, which is available on a loan basis to schools.

The video recording is a natural for musical events. Folk concerts very often happen sort of spontaneously or at least without enough time to get a complicated recording system ready. The portability of the video system makes it easy to record these visually exciting popular music concerts.

Locally, the women's lib groups are using video in their consciousness-raising sessions. They want to document and view themselves at these sessions. It has answered questions like who is overly dominant, how does one physically react to a particular subject matter, what mannerisms are evident, and why are they there in the first place. It would be a good idea if they could watch men interact in similar situations.

Group-encounter sessions are particularly helpful if experienced for

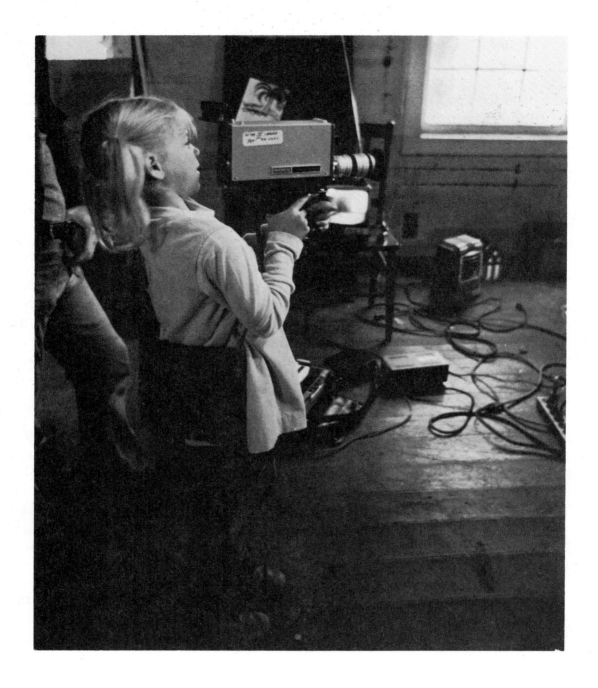

the second time through video. I heard that followers of Janov use video for both group and individual psychotherapy. One person who teaches autistic children has gotten his first real response from certain students through video.

What you can do with video in teaching is wide open. In the first place, because of the simplicity of the equipment, students can use it inside and outside the schools. They can produce their own current-events, dramatic, and historical productions. And on and on.

How-to-do-it instruction will probably introduce the first widespread use of video equipment. Almost anything can be taught through sight and sound. And hopefully the informal approach, which is the right approach, of video will liberate people into happy and productive creativity.

ACCESS TO TOOLS

Looming above all the questions of how to do it, and what programming best serves your needs, is the problem of access to equipment. Although, when comparing film to video and portable video to "professional" TV equipment, the half-inch gear is cheap, that doesn't mean most people can afford to put up the dollars needed to get equipped for the video frontier. So details follow as to where and how you can get hold of video equipment cheap.

Let's start by looking at the typical community and surrounding area. These days there are cable TV systems just about everywhere, and they are a logical first place to look for equipment. Maybe they invested at one time in half-inch gear but couldn't find a way to make it profitable for local origination. Chances are they have keyed their programming to local commercial ventures. Perhaps you can help liberate these locked-up gear-goodies by offering a solid program that will interest the community. Prove that you can sell the show (commercially) or get a sponsor, or maybe you can afford to agree to underwrite the minimal production costs in exchange for access to the equipment. Little by little, the cable people can be nudged into giving you and your group more and more control over the equipment if you play your cards right.

Another vital source is the local school. Most of them have some video equipment now, usually locked up where even the teachers can't get at it. Often there are departments called Instructional Media, or some such, that control all the stuff. Since it was all purchased in the public's name for use in the school system, perhaps you can get access to this equipment by running a workshop for students and teachers. Turn the kids on to video and they'll demand that the equipment be made available to them, instead of being held in some dark corner encrusted with cobwebs.

Local community colleges are a good source of equipment, but it seems harder to open them up. Chances are they have a full TV studio which is empty most of the time. Try to stick your finger in that pie, and offer to organize a course in video for students and faculty. The trick is always to get the gear out of the clutches of the administrators, who are overly worried about breakage and concerned about guarding their unused toys. Problem is, they never want the toys played with at all—unless they can directly control the process. Work through the art department or the humanities people to free up the gear, if you have no luck with a head-on confrontation with the Instructional Media folks.

Other local groups with video possibilities are social service organizations (government and private), such as community action offices, OEO programs, VISTA, United Way, etc. They may have used them in encounter groups, and perhaps they can be loosened up to allow other community groups access.

A real possibility is to band with friends and operate as an organized media group, get community status, and buy or lease your own equipment. Then you can hold public showings on your own monitors, and not have to worry about when and how you can use the equipment. As I said earlier, there already are many video groups around the country, and with a bit of searching you can find one willing to help you get going.

FUNDING YOUR PROJECT

One way to get funding is to set up a community access group and look for government or private foundation monies to support your work. To pull this off, you have to be able to demonstrate that you are already doing something worthwhile, that the thing you want to do cannot be done without their help, and that you are responsive to the community's needs. Also, you will need to show some kind of community monetary or equipment support. Most of these groups are not into funding entire programs, but will help fund part of a project. It's still up to you to show that it can work. Check the local library for The Foundations Directory, which lists foundations that aid the arts and other areas.

Speaking of libraries, check them out to see if they would like to have video demonstrations and projects carried on under their sponsorship. If so, maybe they'd even be willing to front some money to help pay expenses of hardware and tapes.

At the present there isn't any big money to be made in doing half-inch video—as a matter of fact, most outfits in a position to show your work will try to rip it off, saying how pleased they are to let you show your tapes on their system ... nice of them, eh? Remember that if they are a commercial concern, and any tapes you do for them support their organization, it must be worth something to them ...

The more people there are who can swing the financing and be active participants in the relatively low-cost portable half-inch video process, the sooner there will be a major communications breakthrough and the less power over us private television will have.

SOME COSTS

Portable video-tape recorder/playback unit with camera and omnidirectional mike	$1700
Editing deck...	$1400
Monitor (9-inch screen)	$ 225
Unidirectional mike	$ 50
RF unit for portable VTR	$ 55
12-volt standard battery (45 minutes operating time).........	$ 35
Long-life battery pack (3 hours operating time)	$ 120
Audio/video extension cables for camera	$30-65
Special effects generator	$ 600
Camera selector (up to 3 cameras)........................	$ 50
Sync generator	$ 175
Mike mixer	$60-250
Tripod	$ 50
Lights (quartz)...	3 for $150

For the most current information on the rapidly changing field, check: (1) Radical Software Magazine, Box 135, Ruby, N.Y. 12475; (2) Video Exchange Directory, c/o Vancouver Art Gallery, 1145 West Georgia, Vancouver, B.C., Canada.

Needlepoint

Carol W. Abrams

It was the day of the unveiling. The invitation said "formal"—whatever that is. I brushed my teeth and sat on the windowsill to watch a skinny sparrow pick at a clump of dried mud. There had been many secret meetings, with Frank Sinatra crooning through the closed door. The invitation said "formal"? I pulled on my new jeans and tagged a ride. She'd been hiding herself in her tiny studio for months. It had to be something special.

The room buzzed with controlled conversation. Everyone was hungry. Luscious smells floated from the kitchen. There she stood, bright as a poppy in her Lord & Taylor hostess robe, flushed with excitement. It's time. The unveiling. I sat eagerly on the edge of the coffee table. The room hushed as she moved to the double doors and, amid much murmuring and expectant whispers, flung them open. Candlelight and silver warmed the room. And there they stood, eight of them, all matching, carefully arranged to face the crowd, their wood polished to a deep lustre... What was she doing with Aunt Lydia's chair covers? Or were they Maybelle's sister-in-law's neighbor's chair covers? Then again, I thought they might be Cousin Bertram's Cincinnati client's chair covers, or maybe they were the milkman's mother's chair covers... There were gasps. Ahs. "How lovely. She's so talented." "You did it all by yourself? I could never..." Oh wow, there's no room for doubt, I saw those chair covers before—last spring. Ooooh (choke)... that's it! That spring needlework catalogue. Kit #65297J... and the flowers were already worked in! She was saying, "They were a delight to do." Imagine having to say to her grandchildren some day, "Yes, my dears, I colored in the backgrounds all by myself."

I excused myself as tactfully as I could and pressed my way through the crowd. No, I wouldn't be staying. I stepped out of the light and into the dampness of the evening. I was saddened. She had missed so much. The exhilaration of planning and executing her own patterns, the sensuality of choosing her own materials, the excitement of discovery with each new stitch learned. She had missed so very much. Needlepoint, my needlepoint... how I love it. It's a crazy, tension-reducing, soothing, rhythmic, downright addictive new/old craft. It's a way to be alone in a supersociety, giving you a chance to clear your head and concentrate on only the stitching, only the rhythm, only the color, only the terrain to be covered. Best of all, it's not complicated.

With very little equipment, some vision, and very little time you can master and enjoy needlepoint. And, unlike most other needlework crafts, learning the initial techniques doesn't eat up hours. With only one or two basic stitches you can explore new regions of visual space, or you can hit the canvas in coloring-book style. It's so flexible that it covers the whole range in between.

Needlepoint starts with a canvas that looks more like three-dimensional graph paper than canvas and ends up with a solidly filled-in, heavy fabric. Sometimes it's called needlepoint tapestry, because at first glance it looks as if it were woven like a tapestry. Unlike embroidery, where the fabric is as much a part of the pattern as the stitches, needlepoint stitches completely cover the fabric, actually becoming one with it.

Go to a well-supplied needlecraft shop and browse. Really browse; check out canvases, for one thing, but really concentrate on the yarn. Sort of get an idea of what you are letting yourself into. See what you will have available for your projects. Touch the wools and cords, put them next to each other, let their colors sink in, look at all the yarns and stuff—don't

restrict yourself to "needlepoint yarn." Anything you can thread through
a needle might do. Super-raw beginners may want to stick to the classic
wools, while the more adventurous may move into the exotic macrame
cords and such. Just remember—you're browsing right now.

When starting needlepoint, designing a project should be first and fore-
most on your list of priorities. A pleasant sojourn in a needlecraft shop
will arm you with ideas. After that, you will probably know pretty much
what colors and yarns and possibly the size canvas you'd like to work with,
and you can then approach designing with more ease. A sampler is fun and
a useful vocabulary-builder—it can be played with, and gives a place to explore textural possibilities, color combinations, and exotic yarns, strings,
and cords. It's the perfect place to record stitches learned, measure yarn
lengths, and generally doodle around. I am always working on a sampler
of some sort right along with my projects.

For design ideas, go for a nice long, slow walk or sit by a window for
a while. Soak in all you see. Really look. Piles of cement blocks; mari-
golds blinking in a neighbor's garden; empty-lot collages of bottles, cans,
papers, weeds, a butterfly, and rocks; rows and rows of store windows;
purply mountains stacked one behind the other; tremendous glass-skinned
buildings; fences covered with roses and grapevines; cows on a very green
field; a river; a gutter; a couple of dumb pigeons—there are possibilities
everywhere. Look. See. Remember and note carefully. What are your
favorite things? What are "your" colors? Do you like geometrics? Are
you into art deco, do you really, really get into Jean Arp? How about a
dog, a kid, cooking, music, cybernetics? What about the bottoms of your
shoes? Get it?

Take out your box of crayons and some paper and express yourself—
work with what you like, move into colors and lots of spaces. Don't get
hung up with "My, that doesn't look like Uncle George," and don't give me
that garbage about not being "artistic," whatever that means. You dig
being, don't you? You know what colors please you (so they're not Harriet's
favorites, and who cares if she'd never have them?). You know what turns
you on, right? As I said, don't give me that junk about not being artistic.
Freedom is the word. Loosen your head and move out. Get it out on paper.
It's best if you do your drawing about the size you'd like to stitch.

Now you've got it—how to get it on canvas is next. But first you've got
to have the canvas. The number of warp and weft threads per linear inch
(warp threads run the length of the material, weft threads the width of the
material) determines the mesh of the canvas. The range runs all the way
from very large mesh, with only 5 threads to the inch, to teeny-tiny, eye-

Two sizes of
penelope canvas

popping 40 threads to the inch. The mesh is not the only factor in deciding what canvas to use. Needlepoint canvas comes in either of two varieties: mono canvas with single warp and weft threads, and penelope canvas, whose threads run in pairs. I prefer penelope canvas to mono because I can move from a large stitch to a smaller one on one canvas—it's like using canvases of different meshes together. If you can't make a decision as to the mesh canvas to buy, pick a middle range of penelope with 10 threads to the inch. This will let you see the stitches fairly well. It also covers relatively quickly, and you'll get to know what needlepoint is all about. The smaller mesh canvases permit more detail. So choose whatever you need to suit your pattern. If it's your first piece, think about it. Be logical—unless you want to spend years on one piece. The reverse holds true also; it's silly to pick 5-mesh penelope canvas for a tiny piece—you'll just get started and—zap!—it's done. The little demon in my head, though, asks if that's all bad. Just think, it'll be done quick. Okay—I'll concede—it's not so bad and could be rather fun, though limiting in detail. Rug canvas (5 to 3 1/2-mesh canvas) needlepoint has become very popular in this instant-result-craving society, and it's certainly a legitimate form, so move where your head takes you.

Buy as much canvas as you'll need for the size piece you've decided to work on. Add 3 inches more all around the area to be covered for a blocking, mounting, and working edge—and 6 or 8 inches more in length for messing around on (a sampler).

Stitching small on a penelope canvas:
spread the closely spaced warp and weft
thread pairs apart with a blunt needle and
proceed to stitch as usual. The stitches
will be about half the size of the sur—
rounding stitches.

The problem of moving the pattern off the paper and onto the canvas has now presented itself. There are two basic methods I find most useful; one is painting or coloring it on, the other is "following the coded square." For a pattern that has bold areas and well-defined colors and is already the size you want to work up, the painting or coloring routine is fun. You need a sheet of thin, clear plastic. You can find the stuff in hardware stores on wide rolls sold by the yard. Get a good-size piece, a yard by a yard at least, so you can use it over and over again on canvases of almost any dimension. With this you also need crayons, an iron and ironing board, masking tape and/or adhesive tape, and a sewing machine or needle and thread. Set the iron at a very low heat. Tape the pattern down to a table and lay the plastic over it. Tape the corners of the plastic so it doesn't shift. Trim the canvas to size, leaving an excess of 3 inches all around the pattern. Be sure you trim along one single warp or one single weft thread on all the sides so the canvas remains square at the corners. Posi-

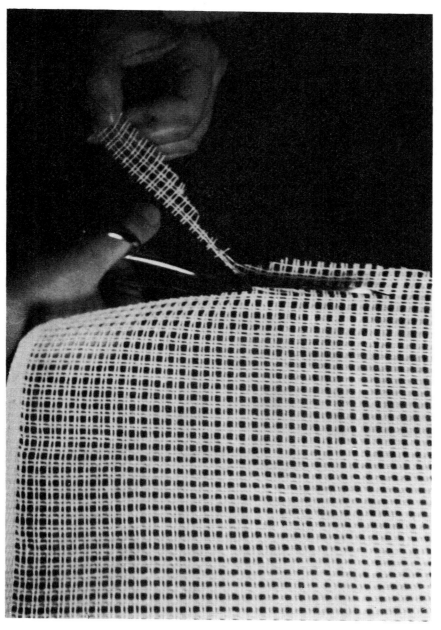

Cut along one single warp or weft thread of canvas to get right-angle corners.

tion the canvas over the plastic and pattern so that the centers of the canvas and pattern coincide. Tape the corners of the canvas. You should be able to see the pattern through the holes in the canvas. With your crayons retrace and color the pattern on the canvas. Remove the canvas from the plastic and place it, face down, on the ironing board. Slip a sheet of paper or an old cloth between the canvas and your ironing board to save the cover from possible staining. Gently press the canvas, using circular motions. (The heat of the iron melts the crayon wax into the canvas fibers, making your pattern permanent and waterproof.) Don't use a steaming iron—it'll stretch your canvas out of shape.

If you'd rather use paint to transfer your pattern you'll need—in addition to your pattern—trimmed canvas, plastic brushes, a palette (an old china plate or ashtray will do), acrylic paints in the colors you need, and water for cleaning your brushes. Acrylics are easier to handle than oils, as they dry in half an hour or so and can be cleaned with water while wet. Tape down your pattern and plastic, lay your trimmed canvas over them, and paint the pattern as described for the crayon method. Mix your paints with a little water if they are very thick, until the consistency is like heavy cream, using your palette as the mixing surface. When your canvas is complete, carefully remove it, and retape it to a flat surface so it stays flat while drying. Clean the plastic and brushes with water before paint dries. Whether you use crayons or paint, save your pattern for future reference.

After the canvas is pressed or dry, whichever the case may be, the edges must be bound to prevent raveling. With my sewing machine I run a long basting stitch all around the perimeter of the canvas about 1/2-inch away from the edge. Then I fold surgical adhesive tape or masking-tape over the edge. Bias tape or grosgrain ribbon can be sewn down over the edge also. This protects hands from being stabbed by the rough, prickly canvas threads bristling out from the edges. It also adds strength to the edges for later blocking. Always follow straight single warp and weft threads while binding the edges, to keep the corners square.

If your pattern has subtle colorations and shadings the "following the coded square" transfer technique is best. This way you get to see pretty much how your pattern will look in needlepoint. The curves you may have in your pattern are broken down into squares on a graph, exactly the way they will be with stitches on the canvas. The advantages of this technique are many: you can enlarge or reduce your pattern on any size canvas without elaborate techniques, and you can very easily change colors consistently throughout your pattern using simple substitution.

You'll need drawing paper, graph paper (found in most good stationery stores), a lead pencil, fine-pointed felt-tipped markers, crayons or colored pencils, and your prepared (edges bound, corners square) canvas. Freely draw your pattern on the drawing paper with colored pencil or crayon. With a dark crayon or marker, outline your pattern's major shapes. Lay the graph paper over the drawing with centers matching. With the lead pencil, lightly trace the pattern on the graph paper disregarding the paper's squares. A draftsman's lightbox or taping the pattern and graph paper to a sunny window would ease the tracing. With felt-tip markers or colored pencils carefully color in each square as it would appear on the canvas. You are

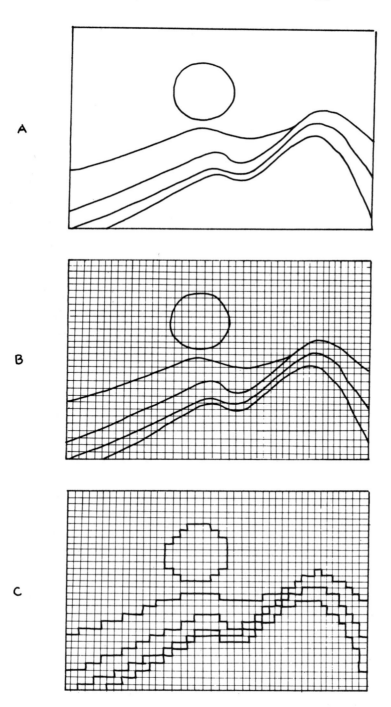

A

B

C

breaking your pattern down into squares, completely square squares; as you can't stitch half a square, don't divide them. If your pattern has very subtle shadings or if you don't like to color, you can code each color with a symbol: orange is ":", red is "/", green is "0", brown is "-", etc. Fill each square that is to be colored with a symbol of that color. This approach is really fine if you happen to change your mind about what colors you are going to use. All you do is substitute the new color for the original and use the same code in working from a chart. Mark the center of the canvas and the center of the chart. This mark will provide a reference point for counting. As you stitch, count the mesh of the canvas, as the holes correspond to the chart's squares, starting from the center and matching yarn color to the code.

⊠ One color   ⊡ A light color
⊞ Another color   ⊠ A dark color
◣ Any color

Needles are basic, and most needlework departments carry a range of needlepoint or tapestry needles. If you are working on large-mesh rug canvas the heftier yarn needles are needed. In all cases the needles are large-eyed and blunt-ended. For the life of me, I can't remember needle numbers, so I have a wide assortment always on hand—something I urge you to acquire. That way you'll be prepared for anything. I can't figure how you can keep the needle numbers straight anyway, they're not printed on the actual needle and I don't know of anyone who can use them without taking them out of the package. If it fits too tight in the canvas it's too big, and if it falls right through it's too small. Easy enough?

The real far-out trip is the yarns. A supreme exhilaration. The colors are lush and the textures deep. Shiny bright silks and pearl cottons and soft, compact English crewel wools for those mini-needlepoint projects; smooth, elegant Persian and French tapestry wools in absolutely stupendous colors and rugged, nubbly rug wools for larger canvases and whatever comes in between. The tapestry wools are the standard wools associated with needlepoint. The color ranges are fantastic. They are strong and easy to work with and give an even, warm, touchable surface to the piece. Persian yarn is the most versatile; it comes three-ply (three strands per length) and can be split to fit a range of the middle-size mesh canvases, the colors are good, and it's available at most places that sell "art" needlework supplies in bulk. The French tapestry wool is a twisted, tough yarn that is fantastically durable and works beautifully for projects that will undergo lots of physical wear. It is difficult to split successfully so it's best to use with the middle-range canvases. Recently a domestic yarn manufacturer has produced a terrific Persian-type three-ply yarn in great colors.

If you are working on a larger mesh size, check out other materials— some macrame cords are beautifully adaptable to needlepoint. Satin-covered rattail and tight, pliable nylon cord, sisal, jute, and seine cordings are interesting. Good old packing or butcher's twine can also be tried. An eclectic approach is most exciting. I say if you can get it through a needle and into a needlepoint stitch, then use it. I use knitting worsteds also. They offer textures and colors I can't find elsewhere and they make an interesting surface next to some other wools and cords. Knitting wools do stretch and shred easily—so don't use long lengths. Some cords are not as flexible as you might like—try using a crochet hook along with your needle. Learning to compensate for whatever problems the "alien" materials may have will make the experience worth much, much more in the long run. Use your imagination. If something doesn't work, you've learned why at least. Biblical-type commandments—thou shalt nots—are not to be obeyed unless you've discovered their practical value. Hell is not in store for a needlepointer who's tried and failed.

The thing that makes needlepoint needlepoint is that the yarn used covers the canvas completely, so fitting the yarn or cord size to the canvas mesh size is a good idea. You can't fit a thick yarn into a small hole, the old saying goes, without just a little trouble—fraying, shredding, and pinched stitches, for instance. Pick up bits and pieces of the kinds of material you'd like to experiment with, along with the classic reliable tapestry wools, and you can mess around a bit on the leftover canvas trimmed off the piece for your project. You'll then know what's good to work up and what you can abandon for the time being.

Bind the edges of the "messing-around" piece and have fun. Try each stitch. Put different yarns against one another. Discover the idiosyncrasies of each yarn. Figure out what yarn you want to use where and get a general picture of what you will use for your project. Work out your problems here.

Determine how much yarn you'll need for your piece by figuring it out on your messing-around hunk. Measure off one square inch on your M. A. (messing-around) canvas and fill it, in the desired stitch, with a measured length of yarn. See how much yarn it uses. Note it down for future reference. Each yarn covers differently, so a notebook listing the type of yarn, the stitch, and the mesh canvas will be of great assistance later. (It's also nice to have for noting design ideas, supply resources, and stitch diagrams.) Measure the length and breadth of the area you want to cover with that stitch and that yarn. It doesn't matter if it's an odd shape—you want a general figure. Take the measurements of the area and convert to square inches. Multiply that number by the length of the yarn used to cover one square inch. Convert this number to yardage and—blare of trumpets—you've got the amount of yarn you'll need for that area. Repeat this process for each area to be filled with different stitches and yarns. Now you don't have to over- or underestimate the stuff you'll need to finish your canvas. Your friendly neighbor hoop & yarn shop is always willing to help. Remember, though, better more than less material, for after all everyone makes mistakes and that loses yarn. Matching dye-lots is a pain. (Make sure everything is colorfast.)

I don't care to use a frame when I needlepoint. I like the feel of the canvas and I find stitching easier without one. Others feel more confident with a frame and say they can see progress better and understand what relationships are developing on their canvases with one. For very large

pieces a frame is necessary, as the weight of canvas and yarn can be difficult to manipulate. In either case, a square frame is perfectly adequate.
These are available in needlework-supply houses and can be very simple,
screw-together wooden slats or very beautiful, floor-standing jobs. You
can make one from four 2 1/2-to-3-foot-long trellis strips from a lumber
yard and four long screws with butterfly nuts. Drill six or eight holes
along either end of each slat about an inch or so apart. The drill bit should
be as big as the screws you'll be using. Staple the unfolded edges of a
folded piece of canvas duck along the edge of two slats (see below).

Needlepoint Frame

To mount the needlepoint canvas in the frame you'll need heavy thread
like that used for braided rugs, and a needle. With the edge of the needlepoint canvas slightly over the edge of the canvas stripping, centers matching, baste the two together with short running stitches. Place the screws
in the holes and tighten with the butterfly nuts. The number of holes in
each slat makes the frame adjustable for different size pieces. If the needlepoint canvas is much longer than the frame, then roll one end over one
of the slats and unroll later when you come to it. (The canvas can be longer
than the frame in only one direction so you can secure the piece in the
frame.)

Now you can stitch. There are many many stitches that have been developed for needlepoint. Because of the restrictions of needlepoint (i.e.,
the canvas must be completely covered, the warp and weft must be wrapped

with yarn, and the canvas mesh itself is angular) most of the "stitches" are simply classic patterns made up of very few actual stitches. Here I have included my favorites, which, as you can see, are very few. What is lacking in number is made up in versatility. I have added a few of the classic pattern stitches to show you that, if you examine them closely, they are just derivations of the few basics. So use your imagination and play with them. You may come up with a new "classic" needlepoint stitch or two of your own.

THE STITCHES

KNOTTING OFF/FINISHING OFF:

A.   From the front insert the needle into the canvas four or five mesh squares away from the point at which you will start stitching. Leave a tail hanging from the surface. Bring the needle to the front of the canvas. On the back of the canvas there should be a long "stitch" spanning the four or five meshes from the point of insertion to the point of the stitching (the broken line in the illustration, next page).

B.   As you stitch, cover over the long "stitch" on the back as you pass the needle through the canvas.

C.   When you reach the tail, clip it off very close to the canvas and continue stitching. This process should be done with each new length of yarn, and, though the Continental stitch is used as an example, the procedure is the same for all the stitches described here.

D.   To finish off, turn the canvas over and push the needle through four or five stitches on the back. Clip the yarn close to the stitches.

A

B

C

BACK

Knotting off/Finishing off

HALF CROSS: Turn the canvas around to work each new row (B). The raw end in (D) is finished off as in the previous illustration.

CONTINENTAL: This is the stitch usually associated with needlepoint. Again, turn the canvas around to work each new row, and finish off as shown on page 204.

BACK

THE GOBELINS:

Basic Gobelin:

A Few Variations on Gobelin:

(A) is a stitch in its own right, and if you use it this way, work it as (C) and (D), but it's also the basis for (E). (B) is worked like basic Gobelin, only you skip every other mesh square. In (E) the rows cross over each other. As Gobelin is worked left to right, there is no need to turn the canvas over to start a new row in a different color. If you choose to use the same color throughout, you can turn the canvas over and reverse the direction of the stitch. Any empty spaces left at the edges are filled in with a smaller stitch running in the same direction as the stitches in the filled area.

CROSS:

REPEAT

EYE: A really fine large filling stitch as a border or as an isolated stitch.

HERRINGBONE: The Herringbone stitch is one of my favorites for background and large-area filling. Each row must be done from left to right, and you should not turn the canvas around to do any of the rows.

MOSAIC: Work this one diagonally. It's interesting done in strips— every other row a new color.

SHAG: To create a thick, ruglike pile, use a crochet hook and short lengths of yarn. Trim to the height desired.

BARGELLO: If you are put down with the whole idea of making a pattern and all that, Bargello stitching is where it's at for you. Sometimes it's called Flame or Florentine stitching, and it works up into designs reminiscent of television interference patterns or an electroencephalogram (remember Dr. Casey?). The first set of stitches establishes the pattern, and you're off into a vibrating growth session: shades of one color growing from light to dark and the reverse, subtle tones of one color with a fantastic slash of shiny cord. Rainbows on jagged mountains. To get an idea of what it's about, play around with felt-tip markers on graph paper and you'll see what I mean.

Bargello (stitches must be vertical)

When you've stitched as far as you care to go, it's time to stop. Stop. Now you've got to finish it off. Zounds! You mean there's more? Blocking is the name of the game, and block we must. Your canvas is probably all lopsided and looking more rhomboid than square. This is the cure.

You'll need a sheet of plywood larger than your canvas, a few old sheets or smooth cloths to cover the board, some rustproof tacks, a pencil, a small light hammer, a pair of household pliers or canvas pliers, Woolite or Ivory soap flakes, a sheet of paper (butcher's paper or brown-wrapping), a right-angle, and a bucket or sink of cold water.

On the brown paper, mark the dimensions that your canvas should be with sides parallel and corners square. Fill your sink or bucket with cold water and swish up some thick suds with the Woolite or soap flakes. Sink your canvas into the bucket and slosh it up and down a couple of times. Rinse _well_ in cold water—soap left on the surface will just attract dirt. Spread the sheets over the board and lay the marked paper over them. Place your canvas, face up, on the paper. It's wet. Match the edges to the penciled outline. With tacks and hammer, tack down one edge, following the penciled outline and stretching the canvas to fit if necessary. Move to the opposite side and, starting from the center of the canvas edge and the center of the pencil line, stretch and tack. You may need a friend to help pull the canvas with the pliers while you tack. Do this on all the sides. Make sure your corners are at right angles. Let the piece dry in place.

The easiest and most universal mounting technique is using canvas-stretcher strips. The strips (get them from an art-supply house) should be slightly smaller than the dimensions of the needlepointed surface. A row or two of stitching should be wrapped over the edges of the strips when you mount, so plan on this when you buy the strips. Once your piece is dry

Mounting

(which may take a few days) remove it carefully from the plywood surface. With tacks, once again, tack one edge of the excess canvas down on the back of the stretcher strips. Then tack the opposite edge, starting from the center out. Do this again for the other two sides. Slip the mounted canvas into a frame and tape or glue brown paper on the back and hang it.

Fantasmagoric visions of tremendous needlepointed ceiling covers, door covers, slipcovers, toaster covers, dog covers, feet covers, book covers, box covers, wall covers, bag covers, birdcage covers, typewriter covers, window covers, body covers, belts, bands, boots, and banners pass through the mind in dizzying succession. Soft, plushy piles interspersed with tight textures. Maybe some beads or mirrors could be fun. Throw in a little embroidery, stitch on leather patches, or a dash of weaving here, a little knitting there. How about cutting some holes in the canvas and mounting another needlepoint, a painting, a mirror, some velvet (can you dig it), or just empty behind? String cords off the edge of the canvas of a needlepointed piece and macrame, or string some beads off them. Picture it done in natural shades. Do up a screen or wall hanging with open spaces to hang pieces of glass, pottery, metal, or bamboo that sound with the slightest breeze.

Need a new knapsack? Make a cover for it in rug wools and tapestry yarns and you'll have one that will last forever. Feels better than canvas to lay your head on and is a pleasure to lug. What about that old bicycle seat-cover? Museums and old historic residences are full of old needlepointed objects. Take a look at them if you can.

Really look at what you see. Do you like it? Interpret it as it strikes you. Get into it, enjoy it, rejoice in being able to see the colors, to feel the textures, to do the stitches. It's a gas to be here.

Got all that?

Fragments

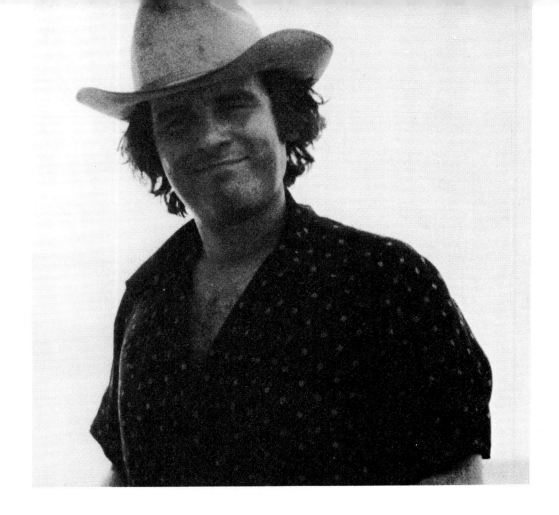

Songwriting

Tim Hardin

The feeling behind the singing of a song may vary from time to time, but the meaning remains the same. The different shapes the song takes will never take the words out of the context or the meaning set up by the first singing.

I write poems and sit down at the piano or play the guitar and sing the words in melodic sentences, using notes that fit the shape of the words and sentences. The melody will rise and fall and twist and turn to the meaning of the words. The delivery of the same song will vary slightly from performance to performance in order to bring straight out the singer's present emotional reactions to the words.

By learning, experiencing, and experimenting with your instruments, vocal and mechanical, you can avoid melodic and lyrical ruts. The more musical expression you have, the less chance you have of repeating the same essence, or a fragment of that essence. To really know that all notes relate to other notes, to really understand the meanings of the words you are speaking, to be free from everything but the pulse and the lyric, means you needn't ever sing the same thing twice. One isn't bound to use the same phraseology for any given tune.

There is no one way to sing a song, except that you should relate to the words and real meaning... over and out.

RUTS

A lyrical rut is an inability to express a new thought right, and it also can be a time when the pencil just doesn't have any more vigor. You want to find words spontaneously that give you the ability to express yourself with nuances outside TV-type dialogue. And the more you understand what you want to say, the more you will be free to escape conventionality.

The same thing applies to melodic ruts; you can fall into a melodic rut by not understanding melodic chordal order. There is order in the building of a melodic essence. This is one way of seeing it. The way I see it.

You can put a strain on a song by _forcing_ yourself to put out. By imposing a quota of musical work on yourself, you may end up with something unreal to yourself. I feel that a song that is really understood has always existed... that's being in tune with the gods.

ON ORIGINALITY

How do you know it hasn't been done? Or does it matter? It doesn't matter. It's impossible to repeat with the same order and emphasis. Even if you thought you were repeating an idea or a melodic essence, you wouldn't be repeating it exactly; something of yourself always comes through, like the individuality of each fingerprint.

There is a lot of plagiarism around, and all real plagiarism is very obvious, especially to the plagiarist. The plagiarist is a party pooper... or the plagiarist hasn't got the poop to party. Don't worry about it unless you _know_ you're plagiarizing, and if you still go ahead... there you are!

Being influenced is different. I think it's been very important in many people's song-writing to have an eclectic source of sound, devices, and so forth.

COLLABORATORS

Many times, a writer of lyrics is at a loss for a rhythmic chordal form for his lyrics. At this time it may be possible for a collaborator to put that melodic essence within the lyricist's sight. For understanding, ask a guy to read the words you wrote and then make a sympathetic background on a guitar or piano: a sky so that you can fly...without a sky, a bird cannot fly. I'll have a guy play a chordal flow that will provide the sky on which I can paint the melody. And that's where it's at with a collaborator for me.

PERSONAL AND COSMIC

The writer is not really an author or composer. He is the one who has gotten in the way of what has always been there and hasn't gotten committed to paper yet. The songwriter commits it to paper with articulation so that what is important is communicated and consumed by the ears and hearts of the listener.

I don't know what the subject matter of a song I write is until I read what I've written. Once again, I'm in the way of the song that's already there. As a writer, you're more vulnerable than the listener to getting in the song's way. The more you're preoccupied with the music, the more you're going to get in the way of the cosmology of the song. I can write songs because I'm a singer. My songs are not personal; it just happens because it is me doing it and it reflects myself. I hope my songs relate something that everyone knows, and that they're "personal" to everyone.

If songs were really just personal, they'd bounce off your neurosis, because your personality would be in the way of anything more universal.

One must learn the magic trick of surrender.

RHYMING

Rhyming is essential. Yes, it is. But rhyme doesn't mean run, fun, sun, bun. The euphony of rhyming can come from the rhythm of the words you are singing. Rhyming makes hearing easy. Just like it's easier to hear music with a pulse. You are reminded of that pulse every time a word has a rhyming sound. There is a reciprocal relationship between the rhyme of the words and the beat. Rhythm is a rhyme, and rhyme reminds you of the rhythm. And that's exactly it.

SONGWRITING

If a line is repeated enough times in a song, people can sing along. In commercial terms, this is called the hook. Or, from another view, repetition is there because it is something that is extra-emphatically important. Sometimes you use repetition at that point when there is an emotional peak, for emphasis ... or maybe for a release at that point when the listeners are ready to sing along.

Repetitious moments usually happen, should happen, at a place that is emotionally right. And every time that emotional part comes around, it is repeated.

Trouble is, everything repeats naturally unless you have enough different parts so that by the end of the statement, the end of the song, you do not have to repeat that much. A lot of my tunes have four parts. It's pulse music, but written in symphonic form; no part is repeated from end to end, like in the "Suite for Susan Moore."

LYRICS

The words make the shape of the song. Both the melody and rhythm of a song are created by its words. The song will always be the same because of the words, and the shape those words make. But it is impossible to repeat any song note for note, because you can never cause the beat to have the exact same length, so the rhythms change every time you sing the song.

Generally, and with me, lyrics come first, before melody, because lyrics are the more restrictive of the two things. Melody is dictated by the shape, order, and meaning of the words. Words are naturally restrictive, and have many syllables. Certain words will not fit with certain other words, therefore; because any musical note may go next to any other musical note of any length, notes and melody are less restrictive.

There is a certain rhythm created by whatever you say, sentence to sentence, word to word. But there are no multisyllabic notes, just one note after another. You can put one note of any length next to any other note of any length. So, it's easier to fit notes to the more restrictive long and short syllables of the words and sentences you write.

The words truly shape the melody, like leaves give body and shape to a tree.

Not every solo songwriter does this, and only occasionally in collaboration. Some apply the words to an existing melody. Such songs are apt to have unnatural sounds. Take Rodgers and Hart. One guy wrote the music and the other the words. Their songs sound very unstraightforward, and they don't really fit. What you're saying in a melody should have very much to do with what you're saying with the words. You want to bring the words into a musical frame of reference.

Something else, though; if a melody is not specifically applied, words may still be sung with their own perfect melody if the singer is able to bring chordal changes into touch with the words.

TIM

How to Write a Song

Robbie Turner

Try your lungs and wings, jump out of the nest with your voice. You don't need any musical training, all you need is something that sounds good or feels good to sing about. If you have ever sung and if you can carry a tune, you need only be aware of what's in your heart, and try to transfer it to voice and onto the wind that gives your voice breath.

Think of letting the words go up and down, tonally, and thrust them out to the air on several different pitches, until you find some notes and patterns of notes and the way the words fall on the notes is a way that you like. If it pleases you, a song might develop. But you have got to sing and not be afraid to sing.

All music is sentiment or feeling and expression of emotions. Singin' somethin' you don't feel or remaining true to a cause that's not happening for you any more and getting overemotional about it while you're singin' is only wallowing in sentimentality. I like to think about an old flame, for instance, and a song about her may really express what I feel at the time. But when you're not into feeling it right, you could be just self-indulgent and gettin' hung up in sentimentality from the desire to write about it.

Some people think that melody is the most important, some say the lyrics are; but I don't think it much matters. Only lack of self-confidence ever kept most of us from doing anything we wanted to do, and where we start is a matter ever-changing.

First, if you know how to play a chord instrument, like a piano or a guitar, already you can accompany yourself. Otherwise, you'll be singin' a cappella (unaccompanied). It's good to know how to play an instrument when you're writing a song because you can voice chords on the instrument and hear how it sounds with music background. Yes, I can admit that eight years of classical training on the cello and four years of symphony training can have a lot of influence when it comes to the technique of playing, knowing the ins and outs of music, the scales and basic knowledge of theory—but I know people who can't play any instrument who have written beautiful songs and enchanting melodies.

The more you keep at practicing singing and developing your talent, or interest in writing (singing is the most important), then the more talent shall be given to you. So keep at it.

Secondly, there's the point of trying to relate what comes first, the chicken or the egg—in musical terms, the lyrics or the melody. Well, sometimes when I'm foolin' around on the piano, or the guitar, I play a lick that strikes my fancy, and it sort of falls into place with some other lick I've played and liked, and I couple the two licks together and presto! the chord structure falls into place for a new song. I may like the movement, or the way that the chords go, and that's all. I can't think of a melody for it just yet. So the song goes unfinished into my back-log and hangs out there till one day I have an experience that (me being a songwriter) gives me a great idea or theme for a song, so I run to my back-log (memory bank), flip the mental pages to that chord structure I recall, and see if it fits the idea or mood I'm trying to convey. If it works—that is, if the chords or mood fit the experience—then I just start trying to sing about what I'm into feeling, and a way of saying it or style of singing it just sort of comes in all at once. Sometimes, after I've been experimenting with different ways to sing of my experience, and after trying several different tunes, I've come up with (or rather it came to me) the melody. Experimentally.

But other times, a certain melody will sort of pop into my mind, and I'll be goin' crazy because I want to make a song out of it but can't find the words. Then, usually, if I just start to fool around with that melody one day, the words will come, sometimes triggered through experience, or just by thinking about it.

Another friend of mine says that a lot of times he writes songs from one phrase, a catchy saying he likes, or a word or group of words that form a title, the title to a song. He says he gets a lot of ideas from just a title or topic to sing about, sometimes from just one word. Of course, there are many ways a song can come about. You may have a poem you like and want to put it to music, and not know how.

If you've got a tune or melody you like but can't find the right words, try thinking of something you wanted to say but never got the chance. It may not come right away, but if you keep singing, actually doing it, the words will come. For instance, a person who's angry about something, such as a man whose wife goes out on him, might write a shout-blues type song to protest the infidelity of women; or vice versa, a woman might protest infidelity or the chauvinistic tendencies of men. Anything will do, if it's what you're feelin'.

A friend of mine said to me, "I like to think of myself singing in a way that would please me if I came to a concert and heard myself as someone else." He likes to please people and to see them turned on and having a good time. And he does turn people on when he sings, and gets them stompin' and havin' lots of fun. And you can, too, if you just think you can.

I have found that the best songs I have ever written, and songs that people have told me they enjoyed hearing me sing most, were songs about love, life, the Lord, and, in general, songs that have a positive nature—that is, songs that sing about good and positive things, things that will bring people up out of the depression they're in, make them happy, give them something good to think about, or at least something that inspires their inner feelings.

But my friend sings, "You'll find the blues round every corner." I know what he's talkin' about. Some people identify with blues—"ah, at least someone else knows how I feel." Blues are a release and an escape from pain, with stark naked truth. Most Black Blues'll bring you up but some blues can really bring you down. It's a mixed bag; blues aren't just about misery. They can be about a lot of other things, too. They start with an attitude or feelin' that has to come from deep inside you. The mood conveyed is almost casually cool, not overly emotional (like opera), but nonetheless humanistic in vision and nature. I tell you about blues because they allow the freedom to express yourself and are a mixed bag of moods, a musical structure most people can identify when they hear it. They can be any emotion you want, happy, sad, funky, or however you feel. They can convey a message of love and peace—"People Get Ready" (Curtis Mayfield). A lot of rock is based on blues and vice-versa, like "Ma Soul Rockin' the Cradle To Comfort the Innocent in Time of Trouble." Blues can be used as a mood through which to express a positive message (as women do wearing colorful dresses), like "let loose, man, and dig yourself."

Music we are influenced by comes from all over the globe, and it is difficult to adopt and adapt it to your own, but it can be done when there is sincerity, when the time is taken to try to communicate with each other. Everybody lives out different life styles. But there's a great ethnic cross-section in jazz and rock groups playing today.

"Sing a song unto the Lord. Praise His name with song. Make a joyful noise unto the Lord, praise His name with the high sounding drum, the low sounding drum, the high sounding cymbal and the low sounding cymbal, the many-stringed instruments, the many-pitched trumpet and the harp. Selah." Psalms. Sounds like a plug for rock-n-roll bands.

I believe that when you are singing about love, you are singing about God. If this is the case, then people like the Beatles, in praising love, were in truth acting out this psalm.

If you have a basic talent or interest, and a little faith, or at least a positive attitude, and a real experience or a valid idea to sing about, you can experiment and come up with a melody or lyrics that will move people to feel the mood you want to express.

Moods have a lot to do with it. Moods (or modes, the classical term) are different kinds of patterns of music, or notes, that suggest different feelings, like sad or happy (minor or major). But if you have one idea, try to build on it, like building a house, finding or making a plan with pieces that fit. Like building blocks or Lincoln logs that stack up on one another.

Take your one idea and try to make it go somewhere, change it, then re-solve it, bring it back home to that same idea. Try to form or build a structure to your song, a pattern or design with changes, and a resolve. If you like continuity, or balance, you might structure a song with a verse, then a chorus, then another verse, then another chorus and then an ending. And of course you can do it entirely different.

Everything I have tried to describe is the opposite of how the products of the hype or commercialism that load today's media, like TV commercials, with "nonfeeling" make people feel when they hear it.

If you choose the most positive and constructive ideas to sing about, then your music will be uplifting, naturally.

Finding what you're feelin' inside you is the basis of the songwriter. Without that there is only musical communication that will be void of the timely soul-identity material that someone like Bob Dylan was able to write. On that basis, go—do it, until you've got the perfect expression for your statement, your feelin' and your ideas. Discovering your feelin's, who you are, what's happenin' will give you the strength to work at songwriting and will be what will make your songs meaningful to others.

Robert C. Turner

Stained Glass

Howard Raab

Most people agree that stained glass is beautiful but inaccessible. The art itself has always been surrounded by an air of mystery, and many think it is about to die with the last of the "old master" stained-glass makers. The fact is that stained glass is very much alive, and a revival is taking place in the homes of individual craftsmen.

There are only three or four studios in New York City now that do church windows. Churches seldom commission work any more, and only occasionally is there a church that wants traditional stained-glass technique used for windows. The studios in the city are down to half their labor force and are half empty. When I go into one of these studios to buy glass for my work, the workers are always questioning me—"Are you busy?" or "Are you working?"—because they are anxious about their jobs. They know that stained glass is practically a dying industry. Today, the interest in this traditional form comes mostly from the individual, and this chapter shows how a person without previous experience and with little investment and a small space allotment can make stained-glass objects as beautiful as the imagination can envision.

I got into stained glass by being in the right place at the right time . . . A friend of mine loaned out his shop to someone who knew how to do stained glass in exchange for teaching him the craft. I happened to be there and I picked up on it. I only learned the basics then, and it took a good two years of meeting a lot of people who do stained glass to pick up more about it. A little bit here and there—and I eventually learned. I had only a few skills, like carpentry and making scale models for architects. I also took baby pictures for a year. That was fun, shooting 300 kids a week for department store promotions, but I was always living in hotels and traveling around. It was mass production, but fun.

After spending two and a half years on Madison Ave. in advertising design, I wanted to do something on my own. I thought that stained glass was the field with the least competition in it, and I thought I might make a living at it. At that time there was no one who did stained glass. Later I found out that not too many people buy it because the expense is high, due to the amount of time it takes in making a piece. I can't tell you that you'll make a living selling it. But it is a great thing for people to do for themselves in terms of personal reward. I teach stained glass, sell some pieces, and trade things I make to other craftsmen in exchange for their work. (Recently, I traded some stained glass for some dental work I had to have done.) And I give it away for presents.

I joined the Craftsman's Marketplace in the city and met a lot of good people there when I got into it. I was working with a girl at the time, and we did well selling to stores and doing craft fairs, but you have to do production work to make any real money from it. We wanted to leave the city and eventually move to Rochester to join a craft commune. I made up my mind to do the stained glass that I liked and not do production work. This girl is still doing production work, making money at it, but I think she has ended up not liking it.

The technique I want to discuss is that of copper and solder, or what some people call the "Tiffany" method. It is most suitable for today's artist/craftsman because of its extreme flexibility and tolerance for error. This method is easy to master and allows for more delicacy than the cumbersome and difficult lead techniques used in most church windows. With copper and solder, you can make beautiful and delicate objects such as small windows, lampshades, jewel boxes, jewelry, and anything else you can think of once you have learned of the possibilities and limitations of stained glass.

Occasionally I'm asked if it wouldn't be simpler to work in plastic. I think that plastic can be very beautiful and useful, but a good deal of it has been used to imitate other materials such as glass. As a result, people have become disconnected from glass and many times can't even tell the difference between it and plastic. The difference is, however, very great. The rich color and qualities of light of stained glass can never be matched by any synthetic, and even a little time spent with it will make this apparent. There are also more practical reasons for using glass that result from its extreme durability. It does not dull or scratch easily, is not affected by the heat of soldering, and has textures and surface qualities that are beautiful even when it isn't colored.

GLASS

Here are the two most popular and easily available kinds of glass to work with. (Look in your Yellow Pages under Glass Suppliers, and in the index at the end of the chapter for addresses.)

Commercial Sheet Glass: This glass is mass-produced in the U.S. and is distinguished by its regular surface texture and even color. Some types have been made that show some color variation, texture, and even bubbles, and these are quite nice. Commercial sheet is useful because it is inexpensive, and its unobtrusive qualities do not interfere with overall designs as more elaborate glass does.

Antique Glass: The beautiful color and handmade qualities of Antique make it very desirable, even though it is much more expensive than mass-produced glasses. The name Antique is used because the manufacturing method is very old, though the glass itself is still made at the present time. The process is very interesting. First the glass is blown into the shape of a large bottle (Fig. 1a). The ends are cut off leaving a cylinder, which is cut down the side (Fig. 1b). Then the cylinder is heated until it unrolls into a flat sheet (Fig. 1c). A certain type of Antique is called "flashed

BLOWN-GLASS BOTTLE

BLOW PIPE

a.

CUT LINE

b.

c.

STAINED-GLASS SHEET

Fig. 1

glass." This is a light-colored or clear-base glass onto which a thin layer or "flash" of another color is added. It is used mostly for reds and oranges, which are very expensive, and some blues. To tell when glass is flashed, take a small piece and hold it up to the light. Looking into the edge, you can see the two layers of glass (Fig. 2). Antique is made mostly in Europe and by only one American company, but still all these kinds of glass are available.

LAYER OF "FLASHED" COLOR

BASE GLASS

Fig. 2

For practice, you will want window glass. You can go to junk yards and get a whole lot of storm windows, or you can go to people who always save big pieces of glass that break in their house. It's better to practice cutting on old glass because it's brittle and harder to cut. New glass is so easy to cut you get fantastically overconfident, but if you want to use it you can go to the hardware store and get pieces that have been cut to order.

There is a lot of glass available, once you start to look for it. But it is difficult to find a variety, specifically of the opalescent glass. The increasing demand for it cannot be met unless the few small factories now producing it get new, expensive machinery. I run into places that are going out of business and get remnants of glass jewels and chandelier parts. Optical companies (listed in Yellow Pages) often have seconds on lenses.

TOOLS AND MATERIALS

Now that you know about glass, you should know about the things you use to cut and shape it. Again, see the index at the end, or try your local hardware store when you set out to buy.

Glass Cutters: There are all kinds of glass cutter on the market. I prefer the common, inexpensive, household glass cutter available at almost all hardware stores for under $1. It is thin, light, easy to use, and cheap to replace (Fig. 3). Diamond cutters are for plate glass and difficult to use on the irregular surfaces of stained glass. There is a tungsten carbide cutter, which is too hard for stained glass, and a cutter with a bunch of wheels that can be rotated, which I think is too big and clumsy but which you may like (Fig. 4). Another cutter, which I use for more delicate work, has a thick wooden handle and a smaller wheel than the common type (Fig. 5).

TAPPER

CUTTING WHEEL

HOUSEHOLD GLASS CUTTER

Fig. 3

CUTTING WHEELS

SELECTOR DIAL

GLASS CUTTER
(Not recommended)

Fig. 4

WOODEN HANDLE

GLASS CUTTER

Fig. 5

Glass cutters should be kept lubricated with light oil or kerosene and should be replaced when dull. I keep a little glass jar filled with oil mixed with kerosene.   You can dip your cutter in while you're using it and also store your cutter in the jar.

Buy the cheapest cutters at the hardware store.   They are the best.   It takes experience to know when the cutter wears out, but this is something you will learn in time.   So change cutters often.

Glass Pliers or Plate Pliers: These come in different sizes and shapes, but all work the same way.   They are used to break pieces of glass that are too small to grip with the hands (Fig. 6).

PLATE PLIERS

Fig. 6

Grozing Pliers: The grozer is another plier and is used to trim the edge of glass.   It has flat insides and is made of soft, untempered steel (Fig. 7).   (You can save money buying a regular pair of pliers instead, which some people find more versatile.)

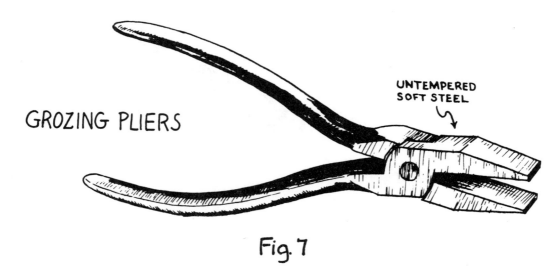

GROZING PLIERS

UNTEMPERED SOFT STEEL

Fig. 7

Hand Grindstone or File: Either of these can be used to clean up rough edges, which make the glass hard to handle. If you use a glass grinding machine, you should wear a dust mask. The glass will be almost powdered and you want to protect your lungs. Hand methods of grinding will not cause a powder and you won't have to worry.

Soldering Iron: This is a very important tool and here quality makes an especially big difference. It should be 80 watts or more, but not over 150 watts, with a fairly large tip. Tiny electrical irons are too slow for the large amount of soldering to be done on stained glass.

Copper Foil: The basis of the structure that will hold your finished piece together is copper foil. It is available as an adhesive tape in a few widths, the most common being 1/4-inch (Fig. 8). However, if you're buying in quantity, you can get a 6-inch-wide roll (not adhesive-backed); you pay for it by the pound, and save a lot.

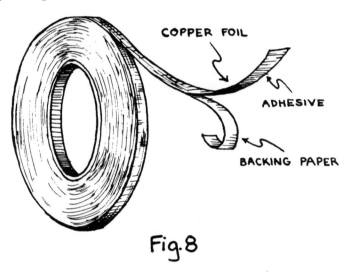

Fig. 8

Solder: A 60/40 grade, 1/8-inch solid-core solder seems to work best for stained glass. The grade means that 60 percent of the solder is tin and 40 percent is lead. Most household solder is 50/50 and does not flow as well as the 60/40.

Good ventilation is very important because of lead content when you're working with solder.

Solder Flux: In order to ensure a clean surface for the solder to adhere to, a flux must be used on the copper. Any plumber's flux will do; however, they are usually difficult to clean off and toxic. There is a soft solder flux available that washes off easily and is not as harmful to breathe. You can get it at Rainbow Studios in N.Y.C. Other places have it, too.

Patina: This chemical, when applied to solder, causes it to turn to a dark brownish color, as in old stained-glass shades. It is certainly not necessary, but I've found it to improve the look of most pieces.

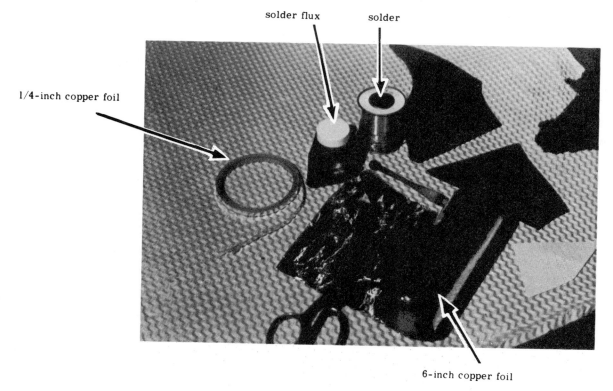

9. Some of the things you'll need

DESIGN AND TRANSFER

Some people who teach stained glass tell people to use ordinary children's coloring books for ideas of simple designing. This is all well and good as a last resort, and to absorb the idea of black lines breaking up areas. Then go home, start making line drawings of anything you like. Nature is full of material, and what you have to do is zero in on an aspect of it and develop it in pattern form. Tiffany was fond of using trees for his inspiration, and the Art Nouveau period is full of leaf patterns, vines, butterflies, and flowers over and over again. The human figure is also a good source to draw from. Arranging different shapes and putting them together in a stained-glass piece is always going to be easy, pleasing, and fun to do.

There are many ways to transfer your design to the glass for cutting. You can lay the glass over the design and trace on the glass with a grease pencil. This is pretty easy when you can see through the glass, but this is hardly ever the case.

Another method is to cut out the pattern pieces from a carbon copy of your original drawing and lay them on the glass. Then you trace around the pattern piece with the grease pencil or use the glass cutter directly, as is done in many professional studios, if you feel confident. The method I use most often involves a light-box. This is easy enough to make and is very useful in stained-glass work (Fig. 10). You lay the drawing on the light-box and the stained glass over the drawing. The light enables you to see the drawing and to trace it on your glass.

If you make a light-box, the glass top should be made out of 1/4-inch clear plate glass. Frosted glass is not really necessary because it cuts off a lot of light and the stained glass itself diffuses light. You want as much light as possible.

LIGHT BOX
Fig. 10

GLASS CUTTING

For a lot of people, cutting glass seems to be the most difficult part of the stained-glass operation to learn. With practice, however, cutting can become almost as easy as drawing.

I don't usually get cut working with glass. You get used to handling glass and learn to keep your fingers away from the edges. However, when

I go out to buy big pieces that I am not used to handling I invariably get some cuts. You <u>can</u> wear gloves, but I don't recommend this when you're actually working with glass, as they mask the sensitivity of your fingers.

When cutting, you should follow the inside of your pencil lines. This will make the piece slightly smaller than the design and automatically compensate for the space later taken up by the copper foil, which you will use after all the pieces are cut and trimmed to the proper size and shape.

Hold the cutter with the flat part between the thumb and index finger and the narrow part resting in the crotch between the index and middle fingers. Try to consider the tip of the cutter as an extension of the index finger. The cutting wheel should always be perpendicular to the glass and the handle tilted back toward you (Fig. 11). You can cut in any direction but it is easier to see what you are doing if you start away <u>from</u> and cut <u>towards</u> yourself.

Fig. 11

Earlier I mentioned a glass cutter with a thick wooden handle and smaller wheel. This cutter is very difficult to hold in the manner just described and so I use a method that is a little unorthodox. I simply hold the cutter in my fist as one would hold a dagger (Fig. 12). This may seem a bit awkward and even childlike at first, but I've found that for small, delicate curves this method gives me more control. The small wheel makes turns easier, and the thick handle fits nicely in the fist.

Fig. 12

Most stained glass is textured on one side and smooth and polished on the other. It is important to cut on the smooth side only. If both sides are smooth, it doesn't make much difference unless the glass is "flashed." Check carefully for flashed glass (see Fig. 2) and always cut the base glass. Glass cutting should always be done smoothly and continuously and never jerkily or unevenly. Pressure on the glass should be firm and constant from the beginning to the end of the cut. Some people tend to press with all their strength, which is not only unnecessary but results in a rough cut-line and lots of broken glass. The scratch should be a thin, almost invisible line, and the moving cutter should sound like a soft whine, not like a

13. Scoring and breaking glass by hand

railroad train.   NEVER GO OVER A CUT.   That is the surest method of ruining a glass cutter and almost never improves the cut.   If you feel the cut is not satisfactory, then make another one elsewhere or turn the glass over and try it on the other side directly under the first cut.

Now, get yourself a big pile of scrap window glass and cut like the devil.   Try to control the cuts by following specific lines and patterns.

After making a cut, the object is to break the glass along the cut line. This, for many people, is accompanied by a good deal of nervousness.

After all, we have been taught the dangers of breaking glass since we were children. The best way to do it, in most cases, is to grip the glass on either side of the cut line and snap down and apart quickly and with confidence (Fig. 13). To overcome your fear of cutting and breaking glass, you simply have to do it over and over again.

Glass acts like a crystal. When you make a scratch in it you are causing a fault. When you put pressure against this fault, it cracks all the way through and the glass is cut through. If you wait <u>too long</u> to break the glass, the scratch will "heal" and the piece will not break right.

If one side of the cut is too small to get a good grip on, then you must use the plate pliers. Place the pliers on the small side of the glass with the front edge against the cut line and, holding the other side in your hand, snap down and away with the pliers (Fig. 14).

Fig. 14

When you are cutting curves, snapping the glass usually does not work very well. The cut line in these cases must be "tapped" in order to break the glass. This is done by using the top end of the cutter, which, in the case of the metal ones, is usually a ball shape. Never use the cutting wheel for this. By tapping the cut line accurately from underneath you will cause the crack to go all the way through the glass and the pieces to separate easily (Fig. 15). Whenever you are cutting a deep, inside curve, it is best to do it in stages. First, make a shallow-curve cut and tap it out. Then keep deepening the cut until it is where you want it (Fig. 16). For outside curves and circles you should also use multiple cuts (Fig. 17).

TAPPER

UNDERSIDE OF CUT LINE

Fig. 15

Fig. 16

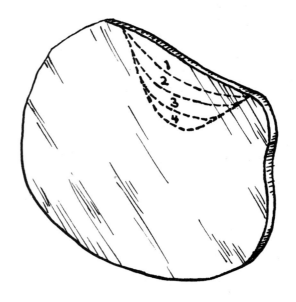

Fig. 17

After you have cut a shape, you may find that it needs some adjustment or trimming to suit your design. For doing this, you will need the grozing pliers which are used to chip away the glass edge. With the tips of the pliers just pinch the very edge of the glass and it will chip off. Do this until the edge is adjusted. Then finish it with the grindstone or file. When you must trim a long straight edge, it is better to use the sides of the pliers as you would use a pair of scissors. With practice, you can alter the shape of a piece of glass very quickly and easily with this tool (Fig. 18).

Now that you have a large pile of broken glass pieces at your feet and it feels comfortable, you are ready to try cutting stained glass.

JOINING THE PIECES

Copper Foil: Using copper foil can be tricky, but dexterity will come with practice. First, peel off some of the foil from the backing paper and start it along one edge of a glass piece, holding it in place with the index finger. The foil should be centered on the edge of the glass. Then continue

Fig. 18

to wrap the foil around the entire piece, folding the overlap down over the sides of the glass as you go. When you reach where you've begun, overlap the foil about 1/4-inch (Fig. 19). You will eventually evolve your own way of doing this, but the result should be neat and uniform. Do this to all the pieces in your design and place them on the original design as you do them. This will keep you from losing track of where they belong. Remove the design before you begin soldering.

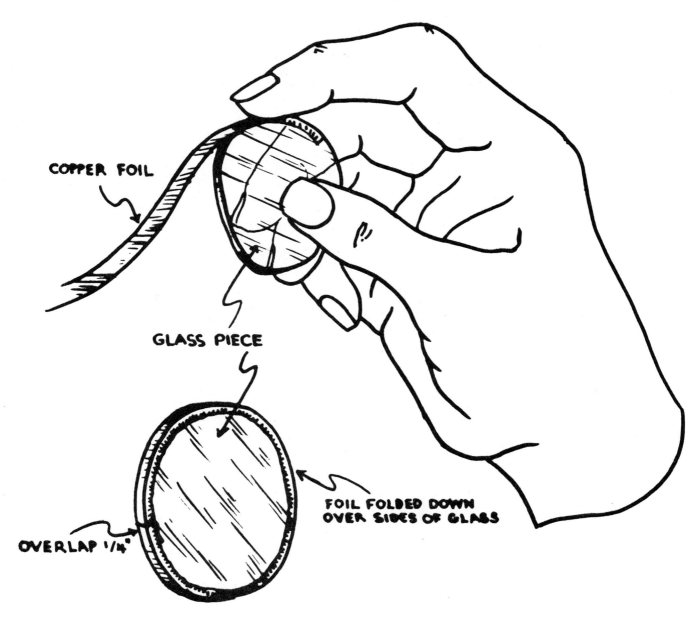

COPPER FOIL

GLASS PIECE

FOIL FOLDED DOWN OVER SIDES OF GLASS

OVERLAP 1/4"

Fig. 19

Soldering: Once the pieces are all wrapped and in place (lay them on any expendable surface—board or even paper), the next step is soldering. You get your soldering tool at a hardware store, and it comes with instructions—basically all you do is plug it in, wait for it to get hot, and then touch the solder with it. With an acid brush apply the flux to all the copper foil showing on the face of the design. Then tack the pieces together at one point where each piece touches another (Fig. 21). "Tacking" is soldering one drop at the joints to hold the pieces in place. Be careful not to move the work while it is being soldered. If this is difficult, then you can keep the pieces in place by putting pins or nails into the work surface around

20. Soldering

PINS

DROPS OF SOLDER

GLASS PIECES

Fig. 21

250

the glass (see drawing). Once the work has been tacked with solder, it may be moved around to make the final soldering easier.

Using a good deal of solder as you go, try to run a "bead" along all the copper joints until they are completely soldered together. A bead is a raised puddle of solder that covers the whole joint (Fig. 22). If there are any open spaces between the pieces of glass, they can be filled with solder if the gap is not too great. Once the first side is finished, carefully turn the work over and solder the other side. After the entire piece is soldered, it must be washed with soap, hot water, and a scrub brush. If the flux irritates your skin, try and find a thin, tight pair of rubber gloves. The flux will corrode the solder if left on.

GLASS PIECES   SOLDER "BEAD"

COPPER-FOIL JOINTS

Fig. 22

You may now use the patina if you prefer. Using a stiff brush, such as an old toothbrush, apply the patina to all of the solder, rubbing it in well. Then, with a rag dipped in the patina, rub the solder until the color is satisfactory. You will find that the color is not very consistent but the over-all effect will usually be good. Let this sit for a while and then wash the piece again, because the patina will form a powder and look bad unless washed off. This time, use a soft sponge or your hands for washing. Steel wool or any abrasive cleaner will scratch or even remove the patina. Your piece is now finished and can be framed or simply hung from a wire loop soldered to a joint at the top.

THREE-DIMENSIONAL SHAPES

The process is similar for 3D-shaped objects, such as lampshades, boxes, sculptures, etc. A mold is very helpful, and many fire- and heat-proof things you find around the house can be used to form interesting shapes. For example, a Chinese wok would be just fine to form a lampshade. The pieces in the design must be small so that they can follow the curve of the mold easily. Otherwise, you must bend the glass, and that requires much different equipment and skills. Just build up the forms on the inside or outside of an object and solder the pieces together (Fig. 23). Be sure that you will be able to remove the piece from the object after it has been soldered on one side (don't use a basket with a handle, etc.). You will be amazed at how much strength the glass form has after it is completely soldered on both sides.

GLASS PIECES BUILT UP AND SOLDERED TO FORM LAMPSHADE

WOK

STAND

NOTE: BE SURE GLASS PIECES ARE CUT SMALL ENOUGH TO CONFORM TO CURVATURE OF FORM !

Fig 23

Glass boxes are simply six flat pieces joined into a box shape with one side hinged if it is to be opened. The hinge can be anything from a store-bought device to simple interlocking wire loops soldered in place (Fig. 24). The top of the box and edges of the lid are edged with copper foil and then soldered.

STAINED-GLASS BOX

HINGES AT CORNERS

WIRE RINGS FOR LEGS

HINGES

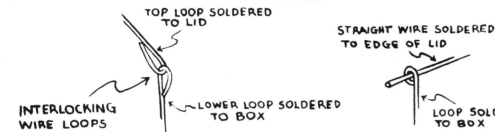

TOP LOOP SOLDERED TO LID

STRAIGHT WIRE SOLDERED TO EDGE OF LID

NOTE: BE CAREFUL NOT TO SOLDER THE WIRES TO EACH OTHER!

INTERLOCKING WIRE LOOPS

LOWER LOOP SOLDERED TO BOX

LOOP SOLDERED TO BOX

Fig. 24

Stained-glass objects can also be done in a freehand manner without using forms. By holding the pieces in place while soldering, you can build up amazing shapes, which can also be combined with other interesting materials. I have used marbles, wire, lenses, and many other things to add interest and texture to things I make.

Once you have mastered the cutting of stained glass and the use of copper foil and solder, the possibilities are endless. Sunlight is probably the best way to illuminate stained glass, but electric lights can also be very exciting.

I would like to do structures that you can sit in or picnic in... environments where stained glass produces light against a background—town, country field or trees, or whatever. Even the biggest churches are stifling to a degree, because you are still between walls. I think that an outside structure lit by stained glass—where you wouldn't even look at the glass itself but at the light being shaped and colored by the glass—would be a very beautiful environment. That's my fantasy right now.

There are qualities glass has that are visual, and tactile, and maybe even spiritual. It responds like no other material and, once mastered, yields great freedom. I've written this chapter hoping that other people can learn to appreciate and make stained glass in order to further its revival and beautify our environment.

SUPPLIERS

Rainbow Studios, Inc.
97 South Broadway
Nyack, N.Y. 10960
- copper foil
- tools
- patina
- flux
Catalogue on request

S. A. Bendheim Co., Inc.
122 Hudson Street
New York, N.Y.
- glass

Glaziers Hardware Products
1689 First Ave.
New York, N.Y.
- tools

Westphal, Henry & Co., Inc.
4 East 32nd St.
New York, N.Y.
- tools

Whitemore-Durgin Glass Co.
Box 2065
Hanover, Mass. 02339
- everything by mail (ask for their catalogue)

Getting It in Print

PREPARING COPY AND ARTWORK FOR OFFSET PRINTING

Rick and Glory Brightfield

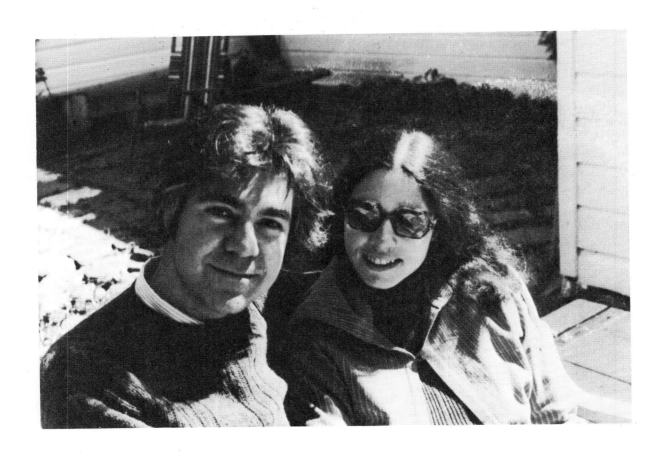

It's easy to sit around rapping about the kind of book or magazine you would like to do. The real thing is to do it. One night Glory and I got the idea for the Woodstock Guide and three weeks later it was printed and we were giving it out to friends. Some stores gave it away, some sold it at 20¢ apiece. We ran out of copies quickly. Glory was half way through her pregnancy, but she still did most of the frantic running around that was necessary to get all the information. While she was doing this, I pitched into the paste-up, and with the help of a couple of friends, one doing the typing (Annie) and the other checking on details (David), we moved fast. We, of course, already knew how to do it, but everything we needed to know is in this chapter.

Just don't get uptight with the relatively few hassles you have to go through. You want to know what you are doing, but learning to prepare artwork, photos, and mechanicals is an easy craft to master.

People have individual reasons for wanting to get their poetry, protests, stories, philosophies, politics, messages, drawings, and other raps out to the public and to friends. The printed page is a good way to spread the word about your individual or collective consciousness.

The form of the material when you give it to the printer determines way it will look when it is printed. What you should give him is a set of "mechanicals." There are a number of things you can do while you're getting it in shape that will save time, money, headaches, and even battles. All of this we will try to lay on you in the hope that getting your thing printed will be an easy ride. There are, however, a lot of technical chores you will have to do. This is because the printers are pretty straight and not into improvisations, so you want everything as clear as a clenched fist.

Mechanicals are ruled-up pieces of illustration board on which the artwork (drawings, photographs, etc.) and type have been assembled in the position you want them to be in. This artwork and type are pasted (or stuck) onto the board with rubber cement, wax, or Scotch tape. For this reason they are sometimes known as "paste-ups and mechanicals," even though a paste-up and a mechanical are the same thing.

The first thing that should be done is to "rule up" the boards. This is done by drawing parallel and perpendicular lines describing the dimensions of the final printed product, be it a book, handbill, newsletter, or anything else. To do this, a drawing board or drafting table is needed.

An inexpensive pinewood drawing board can be purchased at almost any art store. The smallest practical size is 18 inches by 24 inches (and 3/4-

inch thick). This fits on almost any table or desk top and can be conveniently stored away when you are not using it. Since a slightly tilted surface is the easiest to work on when you are ruling up a board, it is a good idea to get a pair of doorstops (the rubber-tipped metal fastenings that keep doors from slamming against the wall) and screw them into two corners of the drawing board. The doorstops can be positioned so you can use the board horizontally or vertically, and they can easily be switched from time to time, depending on the shape of the mechanical you are ruling up.

screw
base
rubber tip
a hook will enable you to hang board up on the wall or in the closet.

Fig. 1

Wooden drawing boards usually have a fairly straight edge on one of the sides of the board. Pick this side for the working side. You can test this (in the store) when you buy the board by sighting down the edge. Hold the board up to your eye as shown in my diagram. If the board has warped at the factory or the store, you will see a slight rise or depression in the surface of the edge.

More expensive drawing boards have a permanent metal edge built into a side of the board. This is usually very straight (but test it anyway).

If you already have a board and the edge is not straight, you can buy a "straight-edge." This is a metal strip with clamps that fasten it to the board.

Fig. 2

When you set up your board at home, you should test it again to make doubly sure that a line drawn with the T-square at the top will be parallel with a line drawn at the bottom. If the distance <u>A</u> is different from the distance <u>B</u> by less than 1/16-inch, you're all right (unless you're an absolute perfectionist).

Other basic materials you will need are one 30°/60°/90° right-angle triangle (preferably one measuring 12" x 6-7/8" x 13-3/4") and a T-square (one having a working edge of at least 18 inches). The T-square and the triangle work together to give you parallel and perpendicular lines (and, of course, right-angle corners).

testing board edge II

tape down
sheet of
paper

draw line
at top

draw line
near
bottom

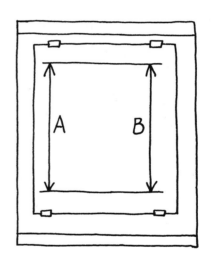

distance A
should
equal
distance
B

Fig. 3

if this happens
get a straight edge. If
you are using a straight edge—
get a new one

There are inexpensive T-squares of wood or plastic that are completely satisfactory. There are also stainless-steel T-squares, which are (over a period of time) worth the extra investment. The latter usually have a minimum working edge of 24 inches, which is a convenient size for working on an 18- by-24-inch raised drawing board.

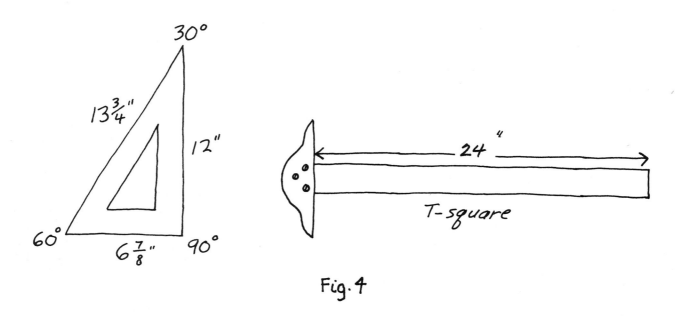

Fig. 4

You will need a bottle (or can) of rubber cement. The smaller sizes usually come with a brush already attached to the top. Also, get a rubber-cement pick-up. This is a small square of rubber that cleans up (like an eraser) excess rubber cement as it dries. There are a few other small things that you will need, like single-edge razor blades, pencils, etc., and these are listed below.

Last, but not least, you will need a supply of illustration board. Start out with a dozen or so 15- by 20-inch sheets of lightweight, "one-sided" (gray back) illustration board. Illustration board comes either "cold-press" or "hot-press." If you are going to do just paste-up, the cold-press is better because it has a tougher surface. It is also slightly rough in texture. If you are going to do a lot of drawing or illustration directly on the board, get the hot-press, as it has a smooth surface and therefore takes ink and other media more smoothly.

blue pencil (Eberhard Faber light blue 2105)

red pencil (Eberhard Faber medium red 2126)

black ball point pen ("BiC")

red ball point pen ("BiC")

a few aluminum push pins ½" point

a "pink pearl" eraser (Eberhard Faber 101)

ruler — aluminum or steel

inches →

picas →

18"

roll of ¾" Scotch Tape

a few razor blades

roll of ¾" masking tape

← brush

small can of rubber cement

pad of medium weight tracing paper 14" x 17"

rubber cement dispenser

large can of rubber cement

Fig. 5

So far we have:

drawing board	$ 6.00
doorstops	$ 1.00
triangle	$ 1.50
T-square	$ 3.00
pencils	$ .60
ballpoint pens	$ 1.00
ruler (18-inch, aluminum or steel)	$ 2.00
Scotch tape (3/4-inch-wide, small roll)	$ 1.00
masking tape (3/4-inch-wide, small roll)	$ 1.00
tracing paper (lightweight, 14-by-17-inch pad)	$ 2.50
illustration board	$ 5.00 (dozen or so sheets 15 by 20 inches)
razor blades	$ .15 (5 at 3¢ each)
rubber cement (medium can)	$ .80
rubber-cement pick-up	$ .25
and a frisket knife (more about this later)	$ .50
Total:	$26.30 (approx.)

This is all the basic equipment you will need. With this you can prepare almost any mechanicals.

If you want to do paste-up on a professional basis, then there are a few more things that you may need, and you may want professional quality in a few items (like the T-square, which can cost up to $15). A hand waxer (which will be described later) is also a good thing to have, but it is somewhat expensive (around $25). Don't worry about these other things now, as you will not need them to start out.

Every job that you do will probably involve some small individual expenses. You may need to buy Artype (which will be discussed) to do the headings. Special pens or brushes may be needed to do an illustration. However, over a period of time you will build up a collection of these things so that, as each new job comes up, you will probably have enough of a lot of things left over from a previous job to make do.

A PERSONAL TOUCH [STATIONERY]

Granted your own stationery isn't the most revolutionary graphic project, but it's an easy one, and since it's personal, you're at liberty to do anything. The printer doesn't care what you do, as long as you square up your board.

1. Cut one of your illustration boards in half (to 10 by 15 inches), using a razor blade and the aluminum ruler as a cutting edge.

2. Tape the illustration board down to the drawing board with a piece of masking tape on opposite sides of the board, or (if you can find a couple) tack it down with two push-pins at the top.

3. Determine the center point and draw a <u>very</u> light, vertical blue line with the triangle (and the T-square).

4. Measure 4 1/4 inches on both sides of the center line and draw two more vertical lines through them.

5. Draw a base (horizontal) line near the bottom of the board (using the T-square).

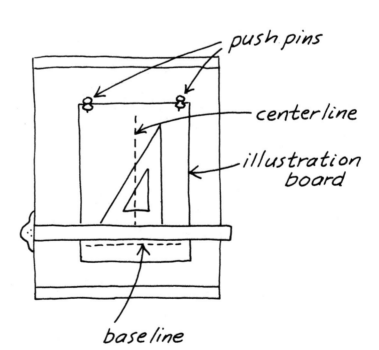

Fig. 6

6. Measure 11 inches up from the base line and draw another horizontal line.

7. Now draw a slightly heavier blue line along the rectangle you have created.

8. All we have to do now is to put "crop marks" at the corners. These should be in black about 1/2-inch long and 1/8-inch from the rectangle. These indicate to the printer that the final job should be trimmed to exactly this size (8 1/2 by 11 inches).

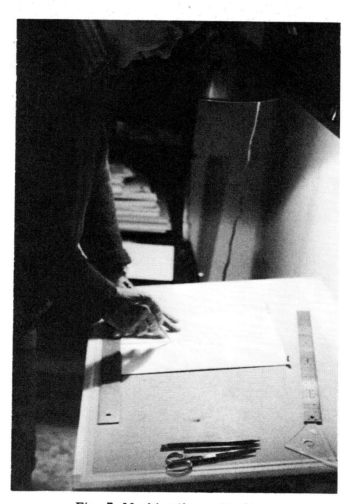

Fig. 7 Marking the center line

The reason for the blue lines is that blue does not show up when the artwork is copied photographically in the process of making printing plates. If, for some far-out reason, your artwork is in blue, the printer can put special filters on his plate camera to pick it up, but under ordinary conditions no blue lines will print. This is why the black crop marks are so important. Otherwise, all the dimensions marked on the mechanical would be lost when it is photographed. Red will also photograph like black. But this color is usually reserved for making "holding lines" (which we will go

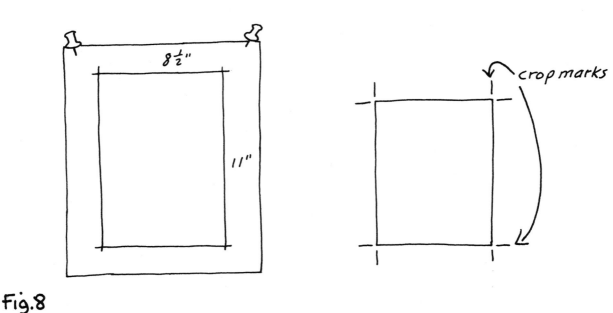

Fig.8

into later). Usually, any black lines within the "live" area of the delineated rectangle will be printed.

Now, since you are doing your own stationery, find some lettering and paste it down. Let's say you have one copy of your old stationery left and you want to get some more printed: you then cut out the type (if it is in red or black) and paste it down in the same position as the original on the new mechanical.

Cut the old lettering out of the stationery. Smear a layer of rubber cement on the board where you want to paste the lettering. Lay the lettering down on top of the glue and line it up (horizontally) with the T-square. When the glue has dried, clean up the excess around the lettering with your pick-up.

old stationery

type

cut out with razor blade or scizzors

make sure lettering is horizontal with T-square

cut edge

smear layer of glue under lettering

rubber cement

Fig. 9

blue line

B

type

C

blue line

distance B should equal distance C

Line up type horizontally with T-square

Use a strip of masking tape to attach a sheet of tracing paper over the lettering to protect it.   The finished mechanical should look like this:

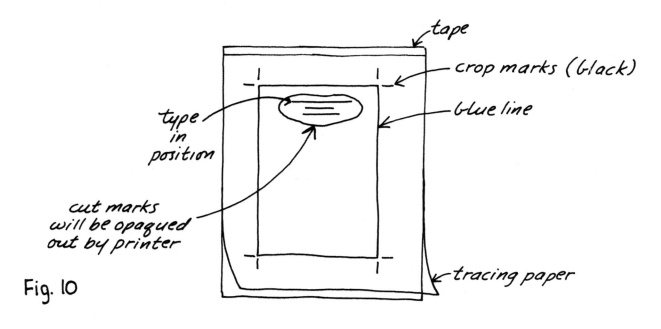

tape

crop marks (black)

blue line

type in position

cut marks will be opaqued out by printer

tracing paper

Fig. 10

This is about all there is to it. This is called a "ready-for-camera" mechanical. It is the kind that printers want to get and it is also the cheapest to get printed.

If you can do <u>this</u> mechanical, you can do <u>any</u> mechanical. Is it really that easy? Well, almost. As someone has said, "You can learn to do a mechanical in an hour, but it takes longer to master the finer points of paste-up." But don't worry about that. If you are going to make your living doing paste-ups, then you can worry about it.

The art of ruling up the mechanical boards and positioning the type and illustrations is the basic craft of preparing copy and artwork for printing. Type, illustrations, etc., will only be printed as well as they are assembled on your boards.

HEADINGS, COPY, AND ILLUSTRATIONS

Most books, brochures, handbills, or posters, etc., contain these three elements. Each element poses its own problems, and then there is the problem of putting them together in a layout so that they will relate properly to each other.

sample from "WOODSTOCK GUIDE"

Fig. 11A

Fig. 11B

The simplest method of producing headings is by hand lettering. This can range all the way from calligraphy, which is done with a flat lettering pen and takes considerable skill and love, to block lettering, which can be done casually with a great deal of freedom and spontaneity.

Block lettering should be done with a good solid black pencil. L.&C. Hardmuth Black 350 No. 2 is a very good and very black pencil; also, a

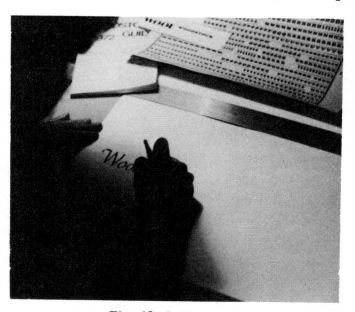

Fig. 12 Calligraphy

black Pentel marker can be used effectively. Be careful not to smear hand lettering with your fingers. For added protection it can be sprayed with a fixative like Krylon.

I am assuming that you are limited as to the amount of money you can spend on any one project. Therefore, you do not want to have "foundry" type set by a commercial typographer. You should, however, know what it is. Foundry typesetting is the traditional process of setting movable type and running a proof of the type on a proof press. This process produces excellent "repros" (short for reproduction proofs of type) that can be easily pasted up. Unfortunately, this kind of heading is very expensive to have set.

You don't have to use foundry type headings because there are several methods of producing headings using sheets of letters that can be cut out and then stuck down, or made to transfer onto a sheet of paper or other surface to produce headings. This takes patience but it can be easily learned.

Woodstock Crafts ← *calligraphy*

WOODSTOCK
WOODSTOCK
Woodstock
} *hand lettering*

← *surface of type*
inked and pressed into
paper to produce a print of
the letter

frisket knife (approx. exact size)

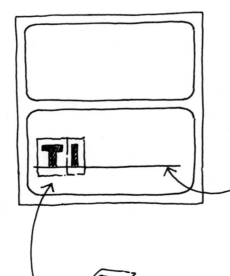

mailing labels
(especially "AVERY"
self adhesive unprinted
labels, 200 labels 2"x 4"
$2.¹⁵ no. 5-6432)

score a line with
the point of frisket
knife

Fig. 13

The two main types are Artype (a brand itself) and transfer type. Letraset and Instantype are two popular brand names of transfer type that are readily available in most big art stores.

One of the best tools to use for both Artype and transfer type is a small "frisket knife." These are usually used for cutting stencils and are very cheap. Frisket knives are razor-sharp when you buy them. For the purposes of moving Artype around or transferring transfer type, these frisket knives should be dulled down by rubbing the sharp edge against a piece of sandpaper until the edge can be rubbed against the palm in safety (don't use your palm to test the blade as you are dulling it).

A good trick is to stick the Artype letters down on a self-stick mailing label. These can be purchased at stationery stores and are used for addressing packages on a typewriter. They are stuck onto the packages after peeling off a paper backing. Cut out each letter from the Artype sheet with a razor blade and carry it with the frisket knife to the label. Be careful not to cut through the backing of the Artype sheet as this will make holes in the sheet, making it difficult to handle.

Score a line on the surface of the label against your ruler with the back of the point of the frisket knife. Use this to line up the letters. Ignore the guide line below the letters put on by the manufacturer as it is not accurate enough. Also, tape the label down to your drawing board and check the horizontal and vertical lineup of each letter.

Fig. 14 Working with transfer type

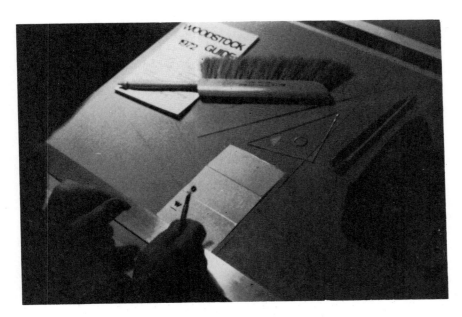

Fig. 15 Cutting out Artype and sticking it on a mailing label

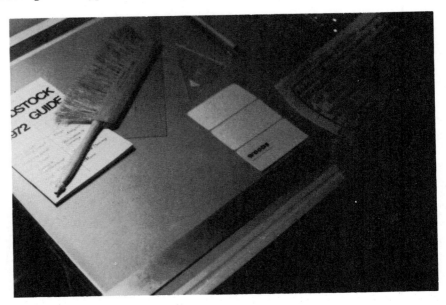

When doing both Artype lettering and transfer lettering be careful about letter spacing. You should always be conscious of the <u>equivalent</u> spaces between each letter. Take the word THE; here the T and the H have to be close to each other while the E is placed a bit away from the H to preserve the equivalent spaces between the letters.

The hardest letters to cope with are A, T, and L. The combination of L and A is very tricky, since it is hard to make up the equivalent space in the rest of the word unless you exaggerate the space between the other letters.

Fig. 16

This will take some practice, but if you keep yourself (at first) constantly conscious of letter spacing, you will eventually do good letter spacing unconsciously.

For word spacing, use about two-thirds the space of a full character (letter).

NOTE: The advantage of having your Artype lettering on self-stick labels will become apparent when you come to do your layout on the mechanical board. If you try to paste down Artype on paper with rubber cement, the solvent in the cement will come through the paper and dissolve the sticky backing of the Artype, and all the Artype letters will move or, sometimes, just fall off. With the self-stick label you can just stick the type down where you want it without the hassles engendered by trying to glue it.

Transfer type does not seem to transfer to mailing labels too well. Transfer type is very fickle about what kind of surface it wants to transfer to. You may have to try a few different kinds of white paper before you find a good surface to use.

To line up transfer type, draw a <u>thin</u> blue line on your paper. Put the letter directly over the blue line (and lined up carefully on the bottom). Then rub down <u>gently</u> with the <u>flat</u> side of the frisket knife blade until the undersurface of the transparent sheet adheres to the surface you're transferring to. Then press firmly down with the <u>flat</u> part of the blade. With practice you can tell by the slight change in tone when the letter has transferred. Then carefully pull off the sheet. Don't press with any kind of pointed or rounded tool, as it will cause the letter to crack or even go to pieces when you pull off the sheet. Besides being a lot of fun once you get the hang of it, transfer type is probably the quickest and most efficient way of producing type headings.

edge of transparent sheet

Line up letter to be transferred

using flat part of knife, rub down over whole area

rub letter until it transfers

Fig. 17

pull up sheet carefully

After being transferred, the surface of the letter is very delicate and can be easily damaged even by gently touching it with your hand. To protect the lettering after you have set the whole word or the whole heading, you can cover it carefully with a strip of transparent Scotch tape.

After you put the tape on the lettering, burnish it down with the flat side of your frisket knife. This makes the lettering fairly permanent. The only caution is that in very cold weather you cannot let the lettering covered with Scotch tape go below freezing as the tape will shrink and crack the letters.

In Figure 11B, the headings were done with transfer type and then covered with Scotch tape. This particular type was "packed," that is, put down so that each (or almost every) letter touches the letter before it. This is one of the many tricky techniques that can be done with both Artype and transfer type, though transfer type is really better for this sort of thing. The A in the middle of the map was put on with Artype.

COPY

The main block of information, that which is introduced by the headings, is called the "copy" (or sometimes "text").

Up until the invention of the linotype machine, most copy was produced by setting hand type in the same way that foundry type is set. Each letter was an individual piece of separate, movable type. The letters were lined up in a handstick (a sort of tray) to form words and sentences and then "locked up" in a frame and used to print directly onto paper. In 1886, Ottmar Mergenthaler first demonstrated his linotype machine (to drag in a bit of history). This machine casts a whole line of type from a row of matrices (or small molds) lined up by typing on a keyboard similar to a typewriter. Molten type-metal (mostly lead with a bit of tin and antimony) is poured into the molds, giving a rectangular piece of metal with the line of type in one piece. A few copies (reproduction proofs) are printed from this type. This kind of type is referred to as "hot-metal" type. As with foundry type, it is too expensive for our (and your) purposes.

The kind of type you will be able to afford is called "cold type," to distinguish it from the hot-metal type described above. There are basically two methods of producing commercial cold type. These are by phototype-setting devices and by the IBM Composer typewriter. At the moment, with a few exceptions, the phototype is not cheap enough to make it feasible for low-budget underground printing. On the other hand, the IBM Composer system is being phased out by IBM (IBM officially denies this but admits that they are no longer manufacturing them). The rumor is that IBM intends to come out with some dynamite system of phototype in the near future that will make all other typesetting systems obsolete. Be that as it may, quite a few small shops, like the Woodstock Times Type Service, have IBM

Composers and produce copy of a very good quality at a price not much greater than typists charge for straight typing.

Cold type is either "justified" (that is, with the lines flush left and right) or "unjustified" (flush left and ragged right). The linotype and phototype systems usually justify the type automatically. One model (a very expensive one) of the IBM Composer also justifies the type automatically: after storing the information from a preliminary unjustified typing, it then automatically retypes the copy, justified. To justify the type on the cheaper model of the IBM Composer, which is still rather expensive, the copy has to be typed twice by hand. This is tedious and not too practical since it doesn't always work the way it is supposed to. So resign yourself to unjustified type. In our opinion it looks better anyway. Most lines of type are justified at the expense of the internal spacing of the words so that, particularly on short lines, you often get exaggerated word spacing.

The IBM Selectric typewriter, though not cold type in the strict usage of the term, produces a very satisfactory type. The Selectric is the machine that has changeable balls, each ball for a different "font," or style, of type. The Selectric, like the Composer, produces a much sharper letter than the ordinary typewriter, since it uses a tape instead of a ribbon, which gives a fabric texture to the letter. Selectric type is particularly effective when it can be reduced (photostatically or in printing) by 15 to 20 percent. The Selectric is now standard in most executive offices and so is often available on an after-hours basis.

The copy in Figure 11B was produced by an IBM Composer typewriter (flush left, ragged right) set in 11-point type but reduced 20 percent. The type on the map was typed on an IBM Selectric typewriter (light italic ball). It was typed onto a mailing label which was cut by word and stuck to the map on the mechanical.

ILLUSTRATIONS

There are two main kinds of illustration that can be used fairly inexpensively in printing. These are "line drawings" and "halftones." Four-color-process illustration, which actually produces all colors using the primaries red, yellow, and blue plus black, is, alas, not for you, unless you win the state lottery. It is very expensive.

LINE DRAWINGS: These are illustrations or drawings that are reproduced from lines and masses of solid black. The final printing is not necessarily in black—this depends on the color of the ink on the press when it is printed. However, the artwork is usually prepared in black. The map in

Figure 11 is a typical line drawing.

The important thing to remember here is that line drawings do not have intermediate gray tones, which must be reproduced either by halftones or Bendays, which will be discussed in a moment. Zip-a-tones, also described soon, are sort of on the borderline, since their gray tones are produced by larger dots than the halftones; however, they can be photographed like line drawings (in technical jargon, "shot as line") if the dots are large enough.

Any medium or technique may be used to create line drawings as long as the areas produced are solid black and white. These include india ink (but not "wash"), black crayon or pencil, or black Pentel marker. The map in Figure 11B was done with a Rapidograph pen.

HALFTONES: These include wash drawings, drawings with Benday tones, and photographs. Halftone is a method of screening artwork or photographs for the printing press during the plate-making process, in which the drawing or photograph is broken up into little dots. If you look at any halftone photograph (that is, virtually any photograph you will see in a newspaper, book, or magazine) under a magnifying glass or small hand microscope, you will see that it is composed of a collection of dots of various sizes. However, they are so small that the eye blends them into a continuous picture of various grays and blacks.

NOTE: You cannot take a photograph that is already screened and use it as a halftone illustration unless the dot is large enough to be shot as line. If you try to rescreen a halftone what you often get is a moiré effect where the superimposition of one screen over another causes an interference pattern, which sometimes obliterates the original.

There is a photographic process called "velox" where the dot itself is large enough to be shot as line by the plate camera. Veloxes are "prescreened" photos or drawings that are done at commercial photo houses and pasted into position on the mechanical, ready for camera. This may save you a great deal of money if you have photos, since the veloxes are much cheaper than halftones. However, the velox screen is heavier (cruder) and will not look quite as good as ones screened by the printer.

BENDAYS: These are areas of solid tone that can be stripped into the plate by the printer if indicated by the artist. For example, if we had wanted to further highlight the map in Figure 11B we could have asked the printer to put a 20 or 30 percent tone of light gray behind the map.

ZIP-A-TONE: These are sheets of cellophane that you can buy in most larger art stores. They have a pattern of dots (grays) printed on one side and a waxy coating on the other side, like Artype, so that it will stick to your mechanical. A line drawing can be made to have areas of tone by rubbing down Zip-a-tone, then cutting around the exact area with a razor blade and lifting off the excess. These areas of Zip-a-tone can be photographed as line.

Zip-a-tones come in all types of dots and textural effects.

SCALING ARTWORK

The ideal thing is to make all artwork the same size as it should be when printed, and to paste or draw it in exact position on the mechanical. However, this is not always practical or possible. Most photographs (except in the case of prescreened veloxes) have to be scaled and then "stripped in" to the mechanical by the printer.

The exact area and position of each piece of artwork and photograph must be indicated exactly on the mechanical with a red "holding line." It is a convention that red is used for holding lines, which indicate the position of artwork only, and that black lines are rules and are to be printed. Again, any black line that you put in the live area of the mechanical will most likely get printed.

In order to scale a piece of artwork or a photograph to the size you want it, you must understand how a diagonal line is used to figure out proportion. In Figure 18, all of the rectangles in the top drawing are exactly proportional.

If you have a photograph or any piece of artwork that has to be stripped in, first determine the amount of the photo you want to include by putting a piece of tracing paper over it and very lightly with a very soft pencil carefully sketching out the rough cropping you want on the final printed photo. It is important not to draw a heavy line with a hard pencil on top of the photo as this will leave a line on the photo, which may show up when the photo is printed.

Then place a heavy piece of cardboard between the photo and the tracing paper, and with your triangle draw in a heavy rectangle over the light preliminary sketch. Remove the cardboard for a moment to check the cropping of the photo. Now, with the cardboard back in place, draw a heavy line from the lower left-hand corner of the rectangle to the upper right-hand corner.

SCALING ARTWORK

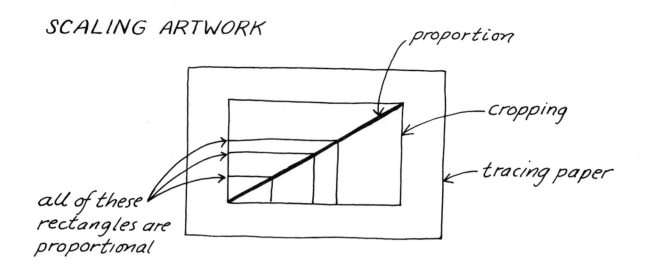

proportion

cropping

tracing paper

all of these rectangles are proportional

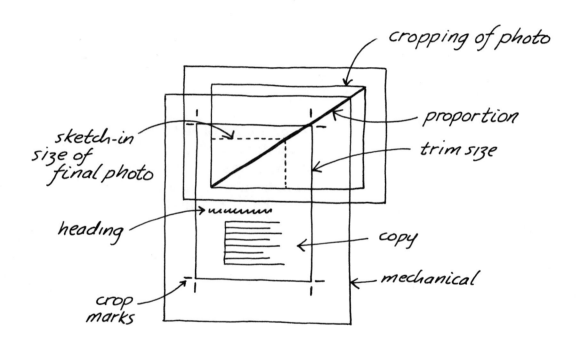

cropping of photo

proportion

trim size

sketch-in size of final photo

heading

copy

mechanical

crop marks

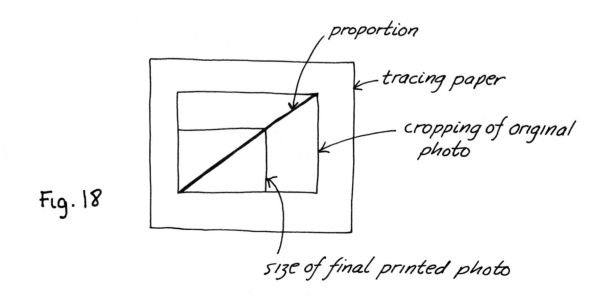

proportion

tracing paper

cropping of original photo

Fig. 18

size of final printed photo

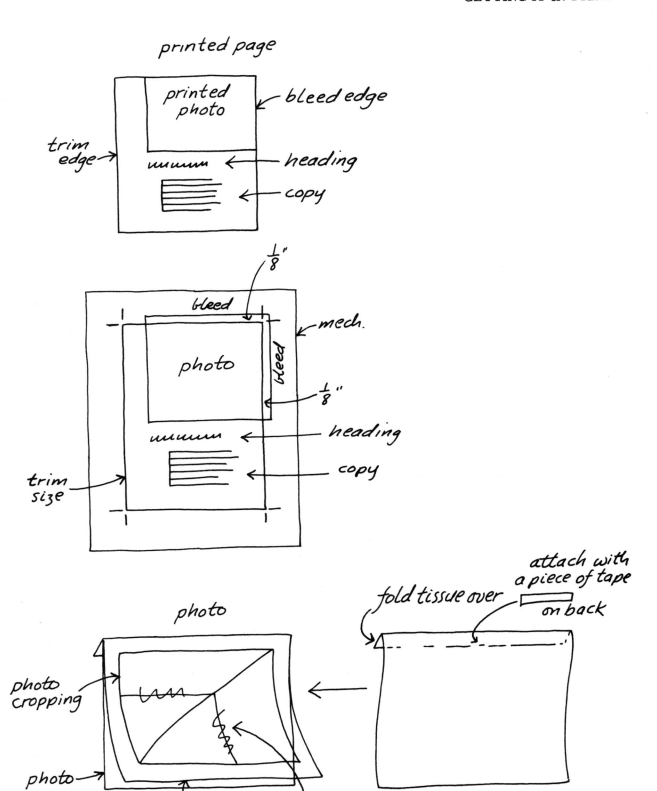

printed page

printed photo

bleed edge

trim edge

heading

copy

⅛"

bleed

mech.

photo

bleed

⅛"

heading

copy

trim size

photo

photo cropping

photo

tissue

erase or cross off

fold tissue over

attach with a piece of tape

on back

tissue

Fig. 19

This is your proportion.

Now, drop the tissue flap on your photo, but do not detach it, and place it over the area on the mechanical where you want to place the photo. Draw in a new rectangle the size of the final printed photo, using the diagonal to keep the same proportion.

Once you have the final photo rectangle, you can move it around over the mechanical to get the exact position. Use a push-pin (or any pin) to make little holes at each of the four corners, through the tracing paper into the mechanical. Use these as a guide to rule in the holding line for the photo on the mechanical. Draw this in with a <u>red</u> ballpoint pen.

Working through tracing paper and using pin holes is a very efficient method of getting exact positionings of all sorts. Pin holes do not show up when the plates are made from the mechanical, and, in any event, will be opaqued out by the plate maker if they do happen to show a bit.

In ruling in holding lines, etc., make sure you always use your T-square and your triangle. All lines should be either horizontal or vertical.

When you have your holding rectangle ruled in, write "strip-in photo" in blue inside the rectangle. All directions such as this should be printed legibly and neatly. Always put yourself in the place of the worker in the printing plant who is going to have to read and interpret your instructions.

BLEEDS

When a photograph or illustration "runs off" the edge of the printed page, this is called "bleed." This is indicated on the mechanical by running the holding rectangle 1/8-inch outside the trim size of the page on the mechanical. This 1/8-inch is later trimmed off by the binder so that the photo runs up to the exact trimmed edge in the final printed page.

Write "bleed" in black (it is outside the live area) in the margin of the mechanical on each side that bleeds.

RUBBER CEMENT VERSUS WAX

Rubber cement has always been <u>the</u> way to glue artwork to the mechanical in commercial art. However, if you are using rubber cement all day, especially in not too well ventilated quarters, it can become very toxic. Nobody knows the long-term effects of inhaling the naphtha (hydrocarbon) fumes from the solvent used to make rubber cement liquid. There is a

RUBBER CEMENT

1. Wet

smear an area with rubber cement

copy

place cut out piece of copy over wet cement

clean

rubber cement pick-up

2. Dry

coat area with rubber cement— let dry

coat back of copy or artwork with cement— let dry

place copy and press down

clean up

3. "One-coat"

mechanical

coat back of copy with one-coat

place on board, in position— press down

WAXER

coat back of copy or artwork with wax

roller

plug-in

place on mechanical

cover with tracing paper

burnish down with edge of triangle

Fig. 20

growing suspicion that it may have some very bad effects on the body. A limited amount of use probably does not have any particularly bad effect, but if you are going to do a lot of paste-up over a long period of time, using wax is a better method.

Up until recently, the only waxing equipment was very expensive and had the further disadvantage of being unreliable. Sometimes the machines just shredded your copy and other times they did you the favor of waxing both sides, which is a sticky proposition.

This situation has improved with the introduction of small, foolproof hand waxers, which are relatively inexpensive and easy to use. All you have to do is place your copy face down on some scrap paper and roll the waxer over the back. This puts a thin coating of wax on the back and enables you to stick the copy down easily wherever you want it on the mechanical. Keep all your scrap pieces of tracing paper as these are very useful in covering your copy while you burnish it down (use the edge of your triangle).

Waxed repros are much easier to pick up again and move around than rubber-cemented ones. You still have to be careful picking the copy up again as it will sometimes suddenly tear if you are not careful.

OFFSET PRINTING

This method of printing has been around for some time, but in the last few years it has taken over the printing field almost completely. Letterpress (locking up movable type in a frame and printing directly with the type, which is also the way reproduction proofs for offset are made from hot-metal type) when it is still used is used mostly for special printing jobs and special effects such as embossing. It is more expensive than and usually not as good as offset printing.

Offset is the only method of printing that is practical for most underground printing projects. Also, this is the type of printing that we have been showing you how to prepare artwork for.

When the printing plate is developed, the areas that have first been exposed to light through a film negative will now take ink. The other areas now reject the ink. The area that takes ink is not raised as in letterpress printing but is even with the surface of the plate. This printing process is often called "planography," that is, printing from a flat surface. It is also called "lithography," since it was first used in printing from a stone surface drawn on with a grease pencil. The stone was kept wet, so that when an

OFFSET PRINTING

board

blue line

black letter

crop-marks

cut edge of paper

black letter reverses on negative

cut marks opaqued out

film negative

crop marks reverse

blue lines do not show up

negative and plate put tightly together in vacuum frame

light

film negative

sensitized plate

plate treated with chemicals (developed and fixed) only exposed area will now take ink

plate put on press

rubber blanket

plate

paper

ink roller

water roller

image printed on rubber roller then onto paper

Fig. 21

ink brayer was rolled across the stone only the grease-pencil lines took the ink. Offset printing uses the same principle. The plate is kept wet and only the areas that have been sensitized by light will take the ink. The correct name for the whole thing is "offset lithography."

This printing surface is much more delicate than a bed of metal type, so that the image must be printed first (or "offset") onto a soft rubber roller, which <u>then</u> prints on paper.

BINDING

The term "binding" is used by printers to indicate everything from trimming and folding to complicated sewn bindings. Forget about the sewn bindings—they are too expensive.

The three kinds of binding that are practical for you are called "side-stitch," "saddle-stitch," and "perfect-binding."

BINDING

8-page booklet, self-cover

all same stock (paper)

←cover stock

cover stock   text

8-page booklet plus cover (=12 pages)

1. Side stitch

staples→

staple on side through all pages

←staple
book will <u>not</u> lie flat

Fig. 22 A

2. Saddle stitch

staples

staples through center of book (or "gutter" as it is called)

staple in gutter

book will lie flat when opened

Fig. 22 B

3. Perfect binding

glue

this binding is always done with a separate cover to cover the glued edge

this permits a "square-back" binding which is useful if you want to put information on the edge (spine)

glue →

information on spine

separate cover

will lie flat when opened

Fig. 22 C

PAPER

Two main kinds (weights) of paper are used. These are "cover stock" (the heavier paper used for the cover of your pamphlet, or whatever, if you need one) and "text."

The most common and popular text paper is called "70-pound text." This term derives from the fact that a carton of this paper (usually 1,000 large sheets) weighs this much. "60-pound text" is cheaper and is also a good paper, but is lighter and thinner.

Cover stock paper is most often "65-pound cover." This term seems to indicate that cover stock is lighter, but in fact it is heavier than text paper. Reason is, a carton of cover stock is smaller.

Also, the more expensive text papers are termed "opaque." This is because they have more filler and the paper is less likely to have "show-through," which is seeing the printing from the other side of the sheet faintly through the sheet itself.

As far as the actual surface of the sheet goes, it can be "vellum," which is a smooth mat surface; a "fancy-finish" (textured), or a "laid" stock, an artificial imitation of old-fashioned paper in which the crisscross pattern of the paper fiber shows.

There is also "coated" stock that has a shiny finish and is the kind of paper ultra-slick magazines are printed on. This is usually very expensive and is also much harder to print on.

For most purposes try to use vellum stock, or "70-pound vellum off-set," as it is usually called. This comes in all different grades, some expensive and some inexpensive. Try to get your printer to find you a job-lot of paper, which is a batch of paper left over from some other job, or paper that was ordered but for some reason not used.

Paper also, of course, comes in different colors. The best thing is to get a sample book of inexpensive and readily available papers from your printer.

SENDING YOUR MECHANICALS TO THE PRINTER

Ways to save money:

1. Make sure you have crop marks on all your mechanicals.

2. Try to have all your artwork as nearly as possible ready for camera.

3. If you can get the "imposition" plan (the way pages are physically lined up when they are printed—this is not the order the pages fall in eventually) for your job from the printer, you can do your paste-up in imposition order rather than in a sequence of facing pages. The printer can usually give you a lower price for the whole job if you do it this way, as he has less work in setting up his plates. Ask the printer about this ahead of time.

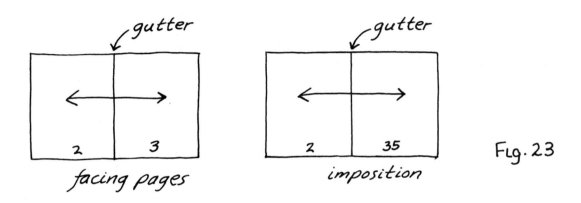

Fig. 23

4. Try to make the size of your job fit the presses of whatever printer you are sending it to. Certain paper sizes fit different presses more economically than others. Your printer will have to give you all this information so that you can plan your job. Make <u>sure</u> you get this information first, before you start ruling up your boards.

Printing costs are, unfortunately, fluid and frustrating, as well as differing greatly from place to place. Most printers want to do a good job for you at reasonable costs. From our experience, this is particularly true of small-town printers, who are very anxious to build business and create confidence and goodwill. In the bigger cities it is advisable to get estimates from several printers in order to compare costs. Many printers will give a "knock-down" price—that is, one with a very small profit, if any—to get your initial business.

Generally, you get a package deal, which includes printing, paper, and binding. The printer will order the paper for you and arrange for binding. You want to establish a good working relationship with your printer, and when you do you can use his advice and guidance.

We hope this will get you working it all out graphically in a new craft...
new to you, anyway. A lot of people who probably never thought they would
be into printing got into it and made it work. The underground press, comics
like Zap and Fritz, political pamphlets, self-help books like the Volkswagen
Manual, books of personal statement like Living on the Earth, newspapers
and magazines like Rolling Stone and the Free Press, ecocommercial catalogues like The Whole Earth, were all done by people who picked up on
printing in order to communicate.

Gloria Brightfield

Rich Brightfield

AB4C